TRUE I.D.

A verse-by-verse study of Ephesians

Dr. Dino Pedrone

XULON PRESS

True I.D.
A verse-by-verse study of Ephesians
by Dr. Dino Pedrone

Printed in the United States of America

ISBN 978-1-60477-492-4

Unless otherwise indicated, Bible quotations are taken from The King James Version of the Bible.

www.xulonpress.com

CHAPTER 1

OUR TRUE IDENTITY
Ephesians 1:1-14

—◌◌—

Identity theft is a problem for so many of us in America today. As we hear of case after case in which innocent people spend months of their lives and thousands of dollars to get their finances corrected, the media constantly talks about identity theft and how can we fix it. There is article after article on that. Here are some safeguards for our protection:

- Photocopy credit card and bank account information.
- Always keep credit card receipts.
- Place a pre-emptive fraud alert on all credit card reports.
- Contact issuers if any new credit cards do not arrive on time.
- For passwords and PINs, don't use the last four digits of your Social Security number, your mom's maiden name, birth date, middle name, pet's name or consecutive numbers.
- Add a second password to your bank account.
- Review bills each month for misuse.
- Shred unsolicited credit card offers before tossing them in the trash.
- Make sure companies lock up your credit loan applications.
- Store canceled checks safely.

Has anybody done all of that? That's what I thought.

It is a full-time job to do all of this. I'm just giving you a portion of what is recommended.

With your spiritual identification, I am happy to tell you that you don't have to do all of that. Consider the wonderful truth about our true identity. If you will take this truth of God's Word into your heart, it will revolutionize the way you look at your life and how you have passion for Christ.

Look at verses 1 and 2 of Ephesians 1. *"Paul, an apostle of Jesus Christ, by the will of God to the saints who are at Ephesus, and are faithful in Christ Jesus, grace be to you from God our Father and the Lord Jesus Christ."*

Notice how the passage begins by saying, *"Paul, an apostle of Jesus Christ."* One of the things we know for sure about the Apostle Paul is that his life was drastically and dramatically changed. His life became absolutely different.

Go back to Acts 22 and, starting in verse 6, Paul is giving his testimony about what the Lord had done in His life and how God was speaking to him and speaking through him. *"And it came to pass, that, as I made my journey, and was come nigh unto Damascus about noon, suddenly there shone from heaven a great light round about me. And I fell unto the ground, and heard a voice saying unto me, Saul, Saul, why persecutest thou me? And I answered, Who art thou, Lord? And he said unto me, I am Jesus of Nazareth, whom thou persecutest. And they that were with me saw indeed the light, and were afraid; but they heard not the voice of him that spake to me."*

Notice what he is doing here. He is giving his testimony.

In Acts 26:12, Paul appears before Agrippa. Here is what he said about his life. *"Whereupon as I went to Damascus with authority and commission from the chief priests, At midday, O king, I saw in the way a light from heaven, above the brightness of the sun, shining round about me and them which journeyed with me. And when we were all fallen to the earth, I heard a voice speaking unto me, and saying in the Hebrew tongue, Saul, Saul, why persecutest thou me? it is hard for thee to kick against the pricks."* And he goes on and tells the story again. What is he doing? He is giving his testimony.

Back in Acts 9 is where we formally find his testimony. Here was this man Saul, on his way to Damascus, and he had in his hand these letters that said that anyone he found along the way who was a Christian would be taken to jail. The account begins in verse 1:

"And Saul, yet breathing out threatenings and slaughter against the disciples of the Lord, went unto the high priest, And desired of him letters to Damascus to the synagogues, that if he found any of this way [whenever you hear "the way" in the Bible, it is talking about Christians because that is how they were referred to at that time], whether they were men or women, he might bring them bound unto Jerusalem. And as he journeyed, he came near Damascus: and suddenly there shined round about him a light from heaven: And he fell to the earth, and heard a voice saying unto him, Saul, Saul, why persecutest thou me? And he said, Who art thou, Lord? And the Lord said, I am Jesus whom thou persecutest: it is hard for thee to kick against the pricks. And he trembling and astonished said, Lord, what wilt thou have me to do? And the Lord said unto him, Arise, and go into the city, and it shall be told thee what thou must do. And the men which journeyed with him stood speechless, hearing a voice, but seeing no man."

What was that? That was Saul's testimony.

Think back for a few moments. When did your testimony begin? A few weeks ago, we had people in our church service give testimonies. It was so dynamic that we could hardly get it stopped, as people told stories of what God was doing in their lives.

When you accepted Christ, immediately you received your spiritual Social Security card. You now have a brand-new identity, and it says that you belong to the King of Kings and the Lord of Lords. Aren't you glad about that today? We are owned, operated by, and belong to Him.

So Paul was saying, "As I went down this road one day, with hatred in my heart to Christians, all of a sudden this light shone down from Heaven, and something happened to me, and that began a brand-new day of identity."

With that in mind, let's look at these verses in the book of Ephesians. We start by looking at the writer of this book: Paul, whose name was changed from Saul.

Philippians 3:5-6 says that he was *"circumcised the eighth day, of the stock of Israel, of the tribe of Benjamin, an Hebrew of the*

Hebrews; as touching the law, a Pharisee; Concerning zeal, perse-cuting the church; touching the righteousness which is in the law, blameless." So he was, according to the Bible, trained as a Pharisee. If you were trained as a Pharisee, you knew religion well. You knew the Old Testament covenant and the Old Testament Scriptures thoroughly.

He was also of the tribe of Benjamin, one of the elite tribes of all Israel. He was a citizen of Rome. Not many Jewish men could claim that, but he was a part of that great Roman empire. Acts 13:9 says that his name was changed from Saul to Paul.

There are many Old Testament and New Testament scholars who say that he could have been named after King Saul. But it is inter-esting that his name was changed to Paul, which means "little one." This reflects the idea of his coming from kingship to understanding who he really is in Christ.

His outlook was changed as well. It doesn't say so in this passage, but often when he writes about himself, he calls himself a "bondser-vant" or a "bond slave." It is the Greek word *doulos*, which literally carries with it the idea of being a slave to Christ.

Notice in Eph. 1:1 how he says he is *"an apostle of Jesus Christ by the will of God."* The word "apostle" here speaks about an office that no longer is in existence, but the term itself means a messenger. In other words, Paul was saved, a child of God and his purpose was to be a messenger.

"For this is what the Lord hath commanded us," he wrote. *"I have made a light for the Gentiles, that you may bring salvation to the ends of the earth."* The man who brought the gospel initially to the Gentile world in full force was none other than the Apostle Paul.

He went through his life fulfilling what God had called him to do, and when he came to the end of his life he said, *"I have finished my course and I have kept the faith."*

Let me ask you something. If you were to die today, if this were your last day to live, what were you on this earth for? You may say, "I don't have a clue." Or, "I know what I'm here for, but I'm not doing very well at it." Stop and think about what you are here for and whether you are fulfilling that.

Paul the apostle said that he was a messenger. He wasn't always sure where that led or where he was supposed to go, but he knew he was here as a messenger.

When God saved the Apostle Paul, He said, "You are saved for a purpose." Imagine as he goes down the road to Damascus. He gets up off the ground, and now he is blind. He was a Jew of the Jews and a Hebrew of the Hebrews, and now he says, "I'm going to be a Christian of the Christians." He really didn't know who he was, where he was going or what it was all about. You see, when you start the Christian life, it really is an ultimate journey.

Now let's look at the city of the book. I love the city mentioned here because it is much like my home city of Miami. In verse 1, Paul addresses this letter *"to the saints which are in Ephesus."*

Ephesus was originally a Greek colony, the capital of the Roman province of Asia, and a very busy commercial center. In the headquarters there was the goddess Diana, or Artemis. The temple was destroyed around the fourth century and rebuilt, and it became one of the seven wonders of the world. People would go there and buy silver statues of Diana and take them home and worship them.

When Paul went to Ephesus and saw this practice, he declared, "This is not what you're supposed to be worshipping." In Acts 19 a riot broke out in Ephesus because of the way he was speaking out against these goddesses and images that were there.

When I think of my home of south Florida, it is a spiritual area but not necessarily a Christian area. We have cults, sects, and all kinds of religions. People are searching, and their search can only truly end when they find Jesus Christ.

Ephesus was like Miami. People were shopping. It was a place of culture, of theaters. Their trademark was the large buildings that were there. Miami doesn't rank in size with Mexico City or New York or Chicago, but when you go from West Palm Beach to Miami, we are a large community much like what was at Ephesus.

The special powers of Diana or Artemis ranged high. Men would go into Ephesus to find prostitution, and it was rampant in Ephesus. One Bible commentator put it very well, and I think it applies also to south Florida, when he said, "The culture was squeezing their spirituality."

Revelation 2 lists seven churches, and the Apostle John is saying something to each one of them. He begins in verse 1 by talking about the church at Ephesus, and the saints that were in the city.

"Unto the angel of the church of Ephesus write; These things saith he that holdeth the seven stars in his right hand, who walketh in the midst of the seven golden candlesticks; I know thy works, and thy labour, and thy patience, and how thou canst not bear them which are evil: and thou hast tried them which say they are apostles, and are not, and hast found them liars ..." (Rev. 2:1-2)

This is a good testimony.

Verse 3: *"And hast borne, and hast patience, and for my name's sake hast laboured, and hast not fainted."*

He is saying some good things here. However, look at verse 4. *"Nevertheless I have somewhat against thee, because thou hast left thy first love."*

Wow. The culture was squeezing their spirituality.

Look back at when you were saved. Consider that moment when you came to Christ. Do you remember how you loved Jesus? Do you love Jesus now like you did back then?

You may have thought, "You know, I'm saved now, so I think I'll just wander through life until I get to Heaven." You need to stop and think: What is your love for Jesus like?

To the saints at Ephesus, Paul said he wanted to tell them about their identity, but in Revelation John pointed out a problem they had. They had gone away from their first love. They didn't lose it, but they left it.

Notice back in the first two verses of Ephesians why that was so serious. It was because they were saints. Paul was not writing this book to the city fathers or community leaders, but he was writing to the saints. Saints are those who belong to God, who have trusted in Christ. These people had two homes: Ephesus and Heaven.

It is interesting that over 90 times in the book of Ephesians we find that little word "in" that means they were "in Christ." Sometimes it literally says, "in the heavenlies," talking about a position we have. We must always remember that we are citizens of two countries. We cannot pursue Christ and withdraw from the world, nor can we become preoccupied with the world and forget that we are in Christ. We are saints.

Some wives may say, "Pastor, my husband is no saint." But if you arc in Christ, I want you to know that God identifies you on your spiritual Social Security card and says, "You are a saint." Say it to yourself a few times. "I am a saint." How does that feel? Not too bad. But do we live saintly sometimes?

Speaking to the saints and the faithful, Paul in verse 2 reminds us that grace and peace are given to us. The word "grace" begins the epistle and is the heart of all that he is going to talk about because we are what we are by the grace of God. A true saint understands that we are what we are because of what Christ did for us.

It is really important for us, as we look at the book of Ephesians, to understand that there is a mystery to this book. What I mean is that God reveals things to us that are not revealed before but also are hard to understand. There is a miraculous-ness to this book.

It begins right away, because in Ephesians 1 you have the Trinity. In verse 3 Paul says, *"Blessed be the God and Father."* That speaks of God the Father.

Verse 7 says, *"In him we have redemption."* Now we have God the Son.

Look down at verse 13. It ends with, *"Ye were sealed with that holy Spirit of promise."*

So in the opening verses of Ephesians, we have the Father, Son and Holy Spirit – three in one.

Someone might say, "Pastor, can you explain the Trinity to me?" My answer would be, "No, I can't explain it, because it is a miracle of God."

You may want to understand things better, but there are some things you and I just don't understand very well. I'm glad God knows what He is about. God the Father is God, God the Son is God, and God the Holy Spirit is God. There is one God.

At the very beginning of the Bible, in Genesis 1, God said, *"Let us make man in our image."* The word "us" there refers to a plurality. Father, Son and Spirit are present from the very beginning. So in Ephesians 1, when talking about our identity, Paul shows how our identity comes from the Father, the Son and the Holy Spirit

11

From verse 3 to verse 12, in the Greek text, is one single complex sentence. We are told the whole concept concerning what God has given us in our identity, when we add verses 13-14 to it.

This brings us to the protection of the saints. If you are saved and in Christ, it is a great place to be. Don't you agree?

Look at verse 3. *"Blessed be the God and Father of our Lord Jesus Christ, who hath blessed us with all spiritual blessings in heavenly places in Christ."* What you need, and what I need, we have in Christ.

Don't ever pray, "God, give me more of Jesus." You received all there is when you got saved. Don't say, "God, give me more of the Holy Spirit." You already have Him. We may need to submit to Him better and yield to Him better. But there is a great truth in this verse, that He has blessed us not with some spiritual blessings, but with all of them.

It is difficult to recognize these blessings, because we identify our spirituality by our daily routine. You get upset at your spouse, and all of your attention is on your spouse. The same goes for whenever you get upset at your children or your boss. Maybe you don't like your neighbor next door because his dog barks too loud at night. We go through all of this stuff down here and say, "You know, this world of ours is such a mess, look at Iraq, etc." Meanwhile, God says that He has blessed us with all spiritual blessings.

Some people smile when they are going through hard times, and some people can't smile no matter what is going on. You know what it's like, because we've all been there. God is saying, "Pull out that spiritual Social Security ID and see who you are in Christ." Let's see what the Father has done for us.

Verse 4 says, *"Just as he chose us in him before the foundation of the world."* I love this thought. There are many people who begin to study the teachings of John Calvin and they become strong Calvinists. John Calvin was a theologian, preacher and philosopher from Geneva, Switzerland. I've been invited to go there and speak and I plan to visit that area. I know people who've been there and they say that many of the people in Geneva used to quarrel all the time about their theology.

The Calvinist says, "God is sovereign, and He saves whoever He wills, and you have no choice in the matter." Then there is the other side, represented by another Bible scholar named Jacob Armenius, who said, "God will save you when you come unto Him, but if you don't hold on, you may lose it." Over the centuries, people have battled between Calvinism and Armenianism, and we almost act like we're God and we know how God did that.

You ask, "Did God choose us?" Yes. If you want to know how He did it, let me give you a profound answer: I don't know. I used to think I knew, but I don't know how He does that.

But I do know this. When He chose us, there was a reason. There was a purpose. Go back to verse 4. *"According as he hath chosen us in him before the foundation of the world, that we should be holy and without blame before him in love."* Why did He choose us? He chose us to be holy and separated unto Him. We are to be blameless. So when God the Father looks at you, and sees you in Christ, He sees you as if you had never committed a sin. He sees you as holy, without blame. Aren't you glad about that? We need to start trying to live that kind of life.

The book of Ephesians is divided perfectly into six chapters. The first three tell us about our identity, and the last three tell us how we should live.

Turn to chapter 2 of Ephesians and look at verse 10. Notice how God speaks to us here about a new life. God chose us to be holy and without blame. Here it says we are His *"workmanship."* God is working on you right now for His glory. Beginning in verse 11 and going into chapter 3, we see a new society that God has called us to. In chapters 4 and 5 we have a new standard that we are to follow – unity and purity. Starting in Eph. 5:21 and going to the end of chapter 6 we read about new relationships and how to get along with your family, your children, your parents, your boss, your employees, and how to stay right with people. This is God's society.

Karl Marx once studied the book of Ephesians and said, "There is a new man," thinking of a new economic society. In fact, this society God is speaking of is His spiritual society

On this earth where you and I live, we will never see peace until the Prince of Peace comes back. We will not see peace upon this earth until Jesus is on this earth.

David Dolan, a leading American correspondent regarding Israel, said recently that there are now five impending wars in the Middle East. This is not a very good society that we live in today. But God's society is all right, because in it you have been chosen and adopted to be the children of God.

Eph. 1:5 says, *"Having predestinated us unto the adoption of children by Jesus Christ to himself, according to the good pleasure of his will."* Why would God go ahead with the creation of the world if He knew it would be followed by the fall of man? According to these verses, it is because He has destined us for something higher than creation would bestow upon us.

In Roman law, adopted children enjoyed the same wonderful privileges as natural children. Being a child of God has rich privileges and demanding responsibilities. My father once said to me, "Just remember, everything you do reflects on your mother and me." Wow. Do you realize that what you and I do reflects on our heavenly Father, on this One who has adopted us into the family of God?

Notice that it says in verse 6 that we are *"accepted in the beloved."* Being adopted means the believer is placed, as a son or daughter, fully into the family of God. It is inconceivable that we should enjoy a relationship with God as His children without accepting the obligation to imitate the Father and cultivate a family likeness.

Verse 6 says, *"To the praise of his glory by his grace by which he has made us accepted in the beloved."* Everybody who has accepted Jesus Christ is a member of the family of God, and they have been adopted into God's wonderful family. When you stop and think about what the Father has done, it's pretty powerful.

Last week I was eating out with my good friend and fellow pastor Jerry Williamson. He and I were talking about things that had happened in the past and people we knew in the family of God. Why would we do that? Because of the relationship we share with the Father.

But we don't stop with the Father. Verses 7-10 tell us about the Son. He gave everything for us. Some of you may have read recently about a man in the New York City subway system who rescued a man he did not even know. The question was asked of others, "Would you do this?" It's a tremendous thought.

Notice in verse 7 the words *"in him."* If that was all we said about Jesus, it would be enough. It says, *"In him we have redemption."* That is a beautiful and powerful word. In Bible times people would be put on the slave block and others would purchase them or buy them back and put them into their families. They would pay the ransom.

The redemption talked about here is *"through his blood."* It speaks about the curse of the law being removed, according to Gal. 3:13. It speaks about being released from the bondage of sin into the freedom of grace, that the Holy Spirit has placed that within us.

My friend, if your sins have been forgiven, put the past in the past. Some of you live your whole lives bringing up the past, and usually with just the bad stuff that happens. Sometimes we bring up the past because we want to tell people how wonderful and good we are now. Some of that needs to go to the past as well.

The final words of verse 7 are, *"according to the riches of his grace."* How many riches does God have? He has them all.

I have about 20 commentaries on the book of Ephesians in my library. One of them is written by the late Ray Steadman of Palo Alto, California, and is called, "Riches in Christ." That's what it is. The message is this: Everything comes to us by Him and through Him, and if Christ is not in control of our lives we don't know if we have the blessings of God or not.

Look back at verse 3 and see where it mentions *"heavenly places."* It also appears in verse 20, as well as Eph. 2:6, 3:10 and 6:12. "Open up your eyes," Paul is saying, "and see what He has given us in the heavenly places."

2 Cor. 4:18 says, *"While we look not at the things which are seen, but at the things which are not seen: for the things which are seen are temporal; but the things which are not seen are eternal."*

There is a great story in the Old Testament about Elisha and his servant. The servant was looking and only seeing the problems. Elisha asked God to open his eyes and when the man's eyes were opened, he saw fiery chariots of God manned by thousands of angels

When we talk about heavenly places, we aren't just talking about going to Heaven someday, but also about having the blessings of the will of God in our lives right now, and we see it and understand it.

You may think that sounds pretty mysterious. Well, the Bible calls it "the mystery of his will." A mystery in Scripture is something hidden that is not revealed. What exactly is this mystery? Eph 1:10 says, *"In the dispensation of the fullness of times ..."* It is important to understand the dispensations of the Bible.

Genesis 1-2 shows the dispensation of innocence. Adam and Eve were placed in the Garden and told what they could not eat. In Gen. 3-6 we see the fall and how they are cast out of the Garden. Sin kept growing until the Flood came, and then in Gen. 12 we have the age of the Promise where God sent Abram on a journey of faith.

In Exodus 20 God gave the law because of the wickedness of men's hearts. Aren't you glad that we don't live under the law today, but under grace?

Now go back to Eph. 1:10. *"That in the dispensation of the fulness of times he might gather together in one all things in Christ, both which are in heaven, and which are on earth; even in him."* That is when Christ comes to take us to be with Him.

God's plan of salvation is always the same, but His method of dealing with people through the ages is different. Just as I deal differently with my four children, God deals differently with each of us.

Look at verse 11. *"In whom also we have obtained an inheritance, being predestinated according to the purpose of him who worketh all things after the counsel of his own will."*

God has given to us the Father and the Son. Jesus died, was buried and rose again for you. That's our Saviour. He provides us the forgiveness of sins.

Verses 13-14 talk about the work of the Holy Spirit. I love what it says here about the Holy Spirit. Verse 13 says, *"In whom ye also trusted, after that ye heard the word of truth, the gospel of your salvation: in whom also after that ye believed, ye were sealed with that holy Spirit of promise."*

God says the Holy Spirit seals you and you are in Him. The word "seal" here is a powerful word that means three things. It refers to a finished transaction, it designates ownership, and it means that you are His possession.

In Bible times, emperors wore large rings that were called signet rings. When one of these rings was pressed down upon a document, one saw that it was a finished transaction, that the ownership was settled, and that it was the emperor's possession. That was it.

When you get saved, you belong to Jesus Christ. That is settled by the sealing of the Holy Spirit.

Verse 14 says, *"Which is the earnest of our inheritance until the redemption of the purchased possession, unto the praise of his glory."* It is the security, or the down payment, with more to come.

Recently I went to a Miami Dolphins football game. I was invited to go. I watched that game from a very special place – the alumni box, where all of the former players sit. I didn't get there because of my looks, or my money, or my position in the community. I was able to enjoy that seat because of Don McNeal, one of our associate pastors who played for the Dolphins in the 1980s. His wife was unable to go to that game and he invited me.

When I arrived in the alumni box at Dolphins Stadium, neither my position, nor my name, nor anything else mattered. The only thing that mattered was that I was with Don McNeal. But I sat there and enjoyed the game, ate the food, fellowshipped with the players and listened to their football stories. (Since I never played football, I didn't have a story to tell.) I was there because of Don.

You have this inheritance, this identification, for one reason and one reason only – because of the work of the Father, Son and Holy Spirit. That's why you are in this family and you have this ID.

Now we come to the privilege of the saints, which is found in verses 13-14. First of all, God provides peace. In the Old Testament, there was the Lord's heritage, the nation of Israel, which was known as God's chosen people. In these verses in Ephesians, both Jew and Gentile have the guarantee of this inheritance. The question is, how do we become God's people? We do so by faith in Christ.

Why do we become God's people? According to verses 5 and 9, it is because of His pleasure. Also, verses 9 and 11 indicate that it is because of His purpose. God willed it. He wants you to be His, and if you will see this fresh view of God, it makes all the difference in the world. You can have peace with God through Jesus Christ.

He also provides purpose. The first three chapters of Ephesians talk about our worth in Christ, while chapters 4-6 talk about our walk in Christ. Chapters 1-3 speak about our position, while the last three chapters speak about our practice, or how we should live. Chapters 1-3 talk about our doctrine and chapters 4-6 talk about our duty. The first three chapters speak about our righteousness in Him and the final three chapters speak about our responsibility.

So He provides purpose, peace and praise. Therefore, we are to praise Him. This passage comes to us in the midst of a violent collision with our world that we live in today. Our world is man-centered and self-centered. We can be imprisoned with our own little egos, almost boundless confidence in ourselves, while God has an insatiable appetite that we bring all of the praise and the glory to Him.

The Word of God will turn you inside out if you let it. It will identify who you are. You will not leave the book of Ephesians with an identity crisis, but you will understand God's new society and what God has in store for you.

You and I are priests of God. We are members of royalty when we come to Christ. You and I belong to the family of God, and it has nothing to do with what you or I did. It's based on the authority of the Father, the Son and the Spirit.

Because of that, it's not a question of whether we should read our Bibles or pray or come to church or try to win people to Christ in our neighborhoods. It's not a question of whether we should be salt and light on the job or anywhere else. If this is your identification, what else would you want to be? How else would you want to live?

I'm so glad for the privileges that God has for us. By the authority of Him, we have our spiritual identification.

CHAPTER 2

EXPERIENCING OUR IDENTITY
Ephesians 1:15-23

_____꿈꿈_____

A re you experiencing your spiritual identification? Are you really experiencing God?

During the past week, for example, perhaps something happened to you that made you stop and think, "Wow, God is working in my life." I believe that, especially in America, we are becoming such a secularized society. God has so much for us but our minds are usually elsewhere and I question whether we are really experiencing God as we should.

The average tenure of a youth pastor in a church is now one year and six months. For a worship pastor the average is two years and six months, and for a senior pastor it is only three years. Obviously, God leads people from place to place throughout their lives, but we need to consider whether there is something else affecting these changes.

Josh McDowell has written a book entitled *The Christian Generation*. He says it is his best book to date. In it he presents the possibility that we are living in the last righteous generation because so many Christians are falling by the wayside. He identifies as a major problem the lack of involvement of parents in the lives of their kids spiritually and in the church. Note that he does not say the lack of overall involvement, but involvement in spiritual matters. He goes on to say that when you survey parents and ask them what are the most important things regarding their children, the top three, in order, are getting a good education, getting a good job and having a good family. The things of God and the church are farther down the list.

If a child is not reached for Christ by age 11, there is a four-percent chance of that child getting saved beyond that, McDowell wrote. Today it is all about relationships, he noted, but those relationships must lead to Christ and there must be substance and value to them. It is a balanced and value-respected relationship that we really need, he wrote.

It is a known fact that some people spend their lives not feeling good about themselves because of something that was said about them, the way they were raised in the home or past experiences. But Paul writes in the first chapter of Ephesians that we are to consider and enjoy the wonderful identity we have in Christ.

There are people in your life you don't like all that much. Have you forgiven them, or are you going to hold onto that the rest of your life? You may look back at a past experience and think, "That was terrible, and I blame so-and-so for letting it happen." Maybe that person was responsible for it, but are you going to keep that bitter thing in your heart from now on?

Look at the prayer of the Apostle Paul that is expressed in Eph. 1:15-23. *"Wherefore I also, after I heard of your faith in the Lord Jesus, and love unto all the saints, Cease not to give thanks for you, making mention of you in my prayers; That the God of our Lord Jesus Christ, the Father of glory, may give unto you the spirit of wisdom and revelation in the knowledge of him: The eyes of your understanding being enlightened; that ye may know what is the hope of his calling, and what the riches of the glory of his inheritance in the saints, And what is the exceeding greatness of his power to us-ward who believe, according to the working of his mighty power, Which he wrought in Christ, when he raised him from the dead, and set him at his own right hand in the heavenly places, Far above all principality, and power, and might, and dominion, and every name that is named, not only in this world, but also in that which is to come: And hath put all things under his feet, and gave him to be the head over all things to the church, Which is his body, the fulness of him that filleth all in all."*

Here is what Paul is saying to us through this prayer: "This is what God has said about your identification, and this is what you have in Christ. Are you experiencing what God says about you?"

Sometimes, as parents, we want to get a point across when disciplining our children and we say things that don't really make sense. I once saw a scene from "The Cosby Show" where Cliff Huxtable took his daughter up to her room and was really letting her have it. He asked her, "Do you understand what I'm talking about?"

With her lip quivering, she said, "Yes."

"How can you?" he asked. "I don't even know what I'm talking about."

That's the way we are at times when we talk to our children. But God is asking His children in these verses, "Do you understand what I'm saying? Do you understand what you have in Christ?" So many of us don't have the right concept of what God really is and what He does for us.

As you read this, imagine that there are four doors on the other side of the room. Behind each door is something God tells us about experiencing our true identity.

As we open Door #1, we hear God say, "I want you to see yourself through your Father's eyes." Look back at verse 17. *"That the God of our Lord Jesus Christ, the Father of glory, may give unto you the spirit of wisdom and revelation in the knowledge of him."*

Wisdom, as it is mentioned here, is the Greek word *sophia*, which is talking about the deeper things of God, the spiritual things He has for us. As important as relationships are, we still need to balance our relationships with the truth.

The word here for revelation is *apocalyptus*, the same Greek word used in the book of Revelation to speak of the unveiling of the future. Paul is saying here, "I want you to open the door and know who God is, and what He is saying about your life. I want you to see yourself through the eyes of the Father."

John 1:12 says, *"But as many as received him, to them gave he power to become the sons of God, even to them that believe on his name."* God wants us to understand that He sees us as His children. Isn't that wonderful?

In Colossians 1:27, He sees us as *"Christ in you, the hope of glory."* In 2 Corinthians 5:17 it is as *"a new creature"* in Jesus Christ. In the book of Romans he declares us *"righteous before God."*

I John 4 says that God loves us with an unconditional love. The book of Hebrews says that we are surrounded by the angels of God, who are always with us.

God the Father says, "I want you to see yourself as I see you."

Verse 17 of Ephesians 1 also mentions knowledge. There are eight verbs in the Greek text that are translated as knowledge. This particular word is *epikinosos*, which means full and exact knowledge and recognition, discerning exactly what God is saying about us.

If you were asked to tell someone the truth about what you were really like, you would probably want to change the subject. God says, "I know exactly who you are and what you are like, and I accept you – through my son Jesus Christ." He has full knowledge of us, and He wants us to know about Him.

My wife reminded me recently that our 40th wedding anniversary was coming up. "What are we going to do?" She asked. Whenever she says that, I realize that she already knows what we will do and she is about to tell me. I know this because I know her.

God is telling us in these verses that He knows us, and He is asking us to consider how well we know Him. He says, "My eyes are upon you." They are the eyes of love, the eyes of compassion.

Door #2 shows us that we can embrace the plan of God. He has a plan for your life. Look at verse 18. *"The eyes of your understanding being enlightened; that ye may know what is the hope of his calling, and what the riches of the glory of his inheritance in the saints."*

In the first part of that verse, God is saying, "Open your eyes." He wants you to see what He has in store for you.

Back in the first verse of this chapter, Paul pointed out that he was writing *"to the saints which are at Ephesus."* As we have already discussed, saints are those who are set apart.

When you look ahead to Ephesians 4, you see instruction concerning leadership in the church. According to verses 11-13,

"And he gave some, apostles; and some, prophets; and some, evangelists; and some, pastors and teachers; For the perfecting of the saints, for the work of the ministry, for the edifying of the body of Christ: Till we all come in the unity of the faith, and of the knowledge of the Son of God, unto a perfect man, unto the measure of the stature of the fulness of Christ."

All of us are to be involved in ministry, both inside and outside the walls of the church. In these verses, God is saying that you are a major player in His work. In your neighborhood or where you work, you may be the best Jesus some people will ever know. How you react when others treat you badly says much about what it means to be identified with Christ and experience a walk with Him.

Author John Piper put it so well when he said, "God has made you for so much more." Scholar Charles Ryrie said the key to this Scripture is "the hope of your calling, the riches of the inheritance, and the great power of God that is displayed through Jesus Christ."

It is easy for us to look around and say, "I can see how God could work in so-and-so's life." But if you are a child of God, He wants to work in and through your life. You have great value to God.

What does God have for you in the next season of your life? Are you getting right in the middle of what God is doing? Are you embracing the fact that He has a plan for you? Often we think about God's plan for the universe and His will for the entire world, but we struggle with His plan for us.

John Wesley was once asked, "If you knew you would die tonight or Jesus would come tonight, what would you do today?" He replied, "I would do what I already have planned." That's a great answer. He said that he would, by God's grace, follow the plan that God already has for him.

Now let's move to Door #3. In embracing what God has for us, the hardest thing for all of us to do is to change something. That's because usually we feel like we're OK. You must believe that God can change you and be willing to let Him do that.

If you are a parent of teenagers right now, you know that everything is about change. If you have an idea, your teenager will come up with what he or she thinks is a better idea. It's all about change, and invariably someone is going to be resistant to it. We have to stop and decide if God wants to change us.

Verse 19 says, *"And what is the exceeding greatness of his power to us-ward who believe, according to the working of his mighty power."*

The word at the end of that verse that speaks of God's mighty power is the Greek word *kratos*, which carries with it the idea of the strength and dominion that belongs to God. We must always remember that strength and dominion belong totally to God.

Another word used here is the familiar word *dunamis*, which is "dynamite" or "the explosion of God." It speaks here about how God can change us and give us the passion we need for His glory.

Josh McDowell has said that parents are involved in children's lives but not so much on the spiritual side. That is so true. You host a school activity and all of the parents come. When you have a church activity, the parents send the kids. When it comes to reading the Bible at home, Dad may say, "That's Mom's job." So how is God going to change us?

I want to challenge you today to realize that, if you're going to embrace God's goodness and what He has in store for you, you will have to let Him change your life.

When you look at the end of verse 19, you see the *"working of his mighty power."* From there it flows directly into verses 20-21, which also talks about the work of God: *"Which he wrought in Christ, when he raised him from the dead, and set him at his own right hand in the heavenly places, Far above all principality, and power, and might, and dominion, and every name that is named, not only in this world, but also in that which is to come."*

God's power seems obvious. But you must ask yourself: Does God have the power to change your marriage? What about your addictions? Can He change your fears or your attitudes toward certain people? Where does this power come from, and how can we get it?

Look at Philippians 2:5-11, a passage commonly referred to as the "emptying" of Jesus Christ. *"Let this mind be in you, which was also in Christ Jesus: Who, being in the form of God, thought it not robbery to be equal with God: But made himself of no reputation, and took upon him the form of a servant, and was made in the likeness of men: And being found in fashion as a man, he humbled himself, and became obedient unto death, even the death of the cross. Wherefore God also hath highly exalted him, and given him a name which is above every name: That at the name of Jesus every knee should bow, of things in heaven, and things in earth, and things under the earth; And that every tongue should confess that Jesus Christ is Lord, to the glory of God the Father."*

The power we have been talking about is the power of the Resurrection. With that kind of power, we must believe that God can change us. One of the most important things about our Christian walk is that we should allow God regularly to change us.

You might say, "Well, I was saved 30-something years ago, and it's been wonderful, etc., etc." But have you been changed lately? In your neighborhood, or at work, there should be something about you that says to everyone, "There is no doubt that he embraces his identity in Jesus Christ."

Sociologists say frequently (especially where I live in South Florida) that there is a spiritual hunger for God, but not necessarily a hunger for Christianity. One of the reasons this need does not always extend to Christianity is that people are looking for signs of Christianity in Christians and not always finding it. We need to live and outwardly show our identification as Christians.

I'm glad that I'm forgiven, chosen by Christ, and predestined to be adopted into His family. I'm glad that God calls me His child. If you are glad of that, then you should live like it and show the world what God says about His children.

Door #4 contains something very important. Look at verses 22-23. *"And hath put all things under his feet, and gave him to be the head over all things to the church, Which is his body, the fulness of him that filleth all in all."*

You need to keep your attention on God's goal for your life. These verses, which show the relationship of Christ (as head of the church) to us (the body) are instructing us to keep our eyes on Christ.

When I lived in the state of New York, I was a pitcher on a fast-pitch softball team. I could throw the ball pretty fast, but no one knew where it was going, least of all me. We had a catcher on our team named David Wood, and he taught me a lesson I will never forget.

"When I squat down to catch the ball," he said, "don't look at the batter, or you'll hit him. Don't look at me. Pretend I'm not even here. Just look at the glove, and throw the ball to the glove." When I began doing that, I did much better as a pitcher.

What the Bible is saying in these final verses is that we need to get our eyes on the glove. In our case, the glove is the head of the church.

The book of Habakkuk has a very interesting thought. The Bible says in Hab. 2:2, "Write the vision." Have you ever sat down to pray about something and then written down what you believed the Lord was telling you? Maybe you scratched part of it out and wrote it again. I recently spent a few days away, praying about the vision for our church.

I believe God is ready for something new in our church, but I also think He has a new vision for the individual lives of every one of our members. The same is true for you and your church. We all need to write the vision.

Notice how those final verses of Ephesians 1 refer to Christ as being *"the head over all things to the church."* This is the first time in Ephesians we find the word "church." Several words are translated in the Bible as church, such as the gathering of fragments or the assembling of a large mass. In this instance, it is the word *ecclesia*, which was originally used to talk about when people would gather to discuss affairs of state. The concept here is that we are gathering to talk about the affairs of God. There is a sense that a large company all over the world is doing this, and when Jesus talked about building His church He was referring to this. But He is also talking about the congregation of believers that make up the local church.

Look at Col 3:1-4. *"If ye then be risen with Christ, seek those things which are above, where Christ sitteth on the right hand of God. Set your affection on things above, not on things on the earth. For ye are dead, and your life is hid with Christ in God. When Christ, who is our life, shall appear, then shall ye also appear with him in glory."*

The words *"seek those things which are above"* and *"set your affection on things above"* could be translated for us today as, "Keep your eye on the goal."

God wants to transform us. What do you believe about yourself, and what do you see yourself embracing? Let's look at these four doors one more time.

Door #1 shows us how the Father sees us. Do you remember when you first became a parent? Of course you do. You show pictures to everyone, whether they want to see them or not. I remember the first time one of my children said, "Daddy." That meant something to me. If I was with my family in a crowded amusement park and someone else's child said, "Dad," I'd turn around and look, thinking they were talking to me. After all, I'm a dad.

This is how the Father looks at us. One of the things Jesus taught when He was on Earth was that God was not just a holy God in Heaven, but He was also our Father. The phrase *"Abba father"* used by Jesus in the New Testament means "Papa father."

At Door #2 we see God's plan for us. Vince Lombardi, who led the Green Bay Packers to five NFL championship and victories in the first two Super Bowls, is regarded by some as the greatest coach in pro football history. He used to tell his players, "We're going to run the same plays and use the same defense. They've got to stop us, and I don't think they can stop us." That's how they won championships. It was a very simple approach, but it was a plan.

Just as Lombardi's players embraced that plan, you and I have to embrace God's plan. As we understand that plan and embrace it, we need to "live out" what God is doing in our lives.

Door #3 is the belief that God can change us. That's the hardest door to look at. Sometimes we don't like to change or confess where we are in our lives.

Door #4 reminds us to keep our eyes on the goal. Keep your attention on Him. As we go through the book of Ephesians, we're going to find out how to have a good home and how to treat other people. We'll study how to pray and help one another, and how to be on guard against the devil. But it means nothing unless you identify who you are in Jesus Christ.

Once when my father was disciplining me, he said, "Whatever you do, don't ever forget that what you do reflects upon your mother and me." I didn't believe it then, but once I had children I knew exactly what he meant.

We must remember each day that whatever you and I do reflects upon Him.

CHAPTER 3

A GIFT OF NEW I.D.
Ephesians 2:1-7

I sat down on the airplane in my middle seat, and a young man sat down next to me. He was huge, probably six-foot-seven or taller. He had a briefcase with him, and he wore a jersey with "University of Maryland" on the front. I noticed that some of his papers contained basketball plays. So I asked him the inevitable question, "Are you a basketball player?" He said that he was, and of course it was obvious who he played for.

So we talked about basketball for a while, and he said, "You know what? We're planning on winning the national championship this year." As it turned out, that was the year they won the national title, the 2001-02 season.

After talking to this young player, I realized that he had a passion for basketball and for winning, and he did just that. With our identification that God gives to us, we have already won the victory in Christ. It's already a done deal.

Back in the days of the Cold War, there was a fear in America of the Soviet Union using its nuclear capabilities against us. Ronald Reagan was elected president in 1980, and by that time he had already spent many years fighting Communism, even dating back to his days in Hollywood as a young man. He was dead sure that he could stop the Soviet threat.

One day he was asked by a newspaper reporter, "What is your strategy for winning the Cold War?"

President Reagan replied, "It's really easy. We win, and they lose."

As a child of God, if you know Christ, you are already on the winning team. This passage tells us to live like we're on the winning team.

Let's look at verses 1-7 of Ephesians 2.

"And you hath he quickened, who were dead in trespasses and sins; Wherein in time past ye walked according to the course of this world, according to the prince of the power of the air, the spirit that now worketh in the children of disobedience: Among whom also we all had our conversation in times past in the lusts of our flesh, fulfilling the desires of the flesh and of the mind; and were by nature the children of wrath, even as others. But God, who is rich in mercy, for his great love wherewith he loved us, Even when we were dead in sins, hath quickened us together with Christ, (by grace ye are saved;) And hath raised us up together, and made us sit together in heavenly places in Christ Jesus: That in the ages to come he might shew the exceeding riches of his grace in his kindness toward us through Christ Jesus."

God has given us a strategy for absolute victory. So far we have looked at the fact that God has given us the marvelous gift of grace, and now I want you to look with me at the idea of transformation, the metamorphosis that takes place when you become a child of God.

The Apostle Paul, who was known as the "Messenger," was writing to the port city of Ephesus, which was much like the current port city of Miami, and was telling them that the culture was squeezing their spirituality.

In Ephesians 1 we find that God had a message for them that was threefold: the Father has adopted them, the Son has redeemed and forgiven them, and the Holy Spirit has sealed them. We have also seen from that chapter that the Father's eyes are looking at us, so we should embrace the plan of God and believe that He can change us and keep our attention on the vision that He has given us.

As we approach chapter 2, here is an interesting thought. You could say that on one side of this passage we find some really bad news. On the other side, we have some amazingly good news. In one part we are, in a sense, in a valley of despair, and in the second part we find that we are going to the pinnacle of hope. On one side is the valley of defeat and on the other side is the mountain of blessing.

The first three verses take us right down into this valley of despair because right away we see a problem. In verse 1 as well as verse 5, it says that we have been made alive. God is saying here that we are alive, there is a life to be lived, He has made us alive together, but the latter part of verse 1 shows that we were *"dead in trespasses and sins."* The problem is that we have been dead in our sins.

What does that mean? In the first book of the Bible, the book of Genesis, in the second chapter, God said to Adam when He placed him in the Garden of Eden that this beautiful garden that he would live in was to enjoy, but He also gave him a warning in Gen. 2:17. *"But of the tree of the knowledge of good and evil, thou shalt not eat of it: for in the day that thou eatest thereof thou shalt surely die."*

This is repeated in the next chapter, as Eve tells the serpent of God's warning in Gen. 3:2-3. *"And the woman said unto the serpent, We may eat of the fruit of the trees of the garden: But of the fruit of the tree which is in the midst of the garden, God hath said, Ye shall not eat of it, neither shall ye touch it, lest ye die."* God did not tell them they could not touch it, but the warning is clear nonetheless.

In the next two verses the serpent responds. *"And the serpent said unto the woman, Ye shall not surely die: For God doth know that in the day ye eat thereof, then your eyes shall be opened, and ye shall be as gods, knowing good and evil."* Satan told Adam and Eve that if they ate of that tree, they would be just like God. We all know what happened next. They chose to eat of the tree, and the result was death.

What is this death? First of all, death is not annihilation. I often go to funerals on behalf of members of our church. At a funeral, you look in the casket and see a body. But death is not annihilation; it is separation. Physically, when you and I die, the body goes back into the ground, ashes to ashes, dust to dust, just as the Bible says.

But the person you really are, the soul, goes on. If that soul goes on to be with God, then you are in the presence of the Lord forever. The soul leaving the body is physical death, but if you are separated from God forever in Hell, that is spiritual death and eternal death.

So death is not an end, but a separation. As Eph. 2:1 says, *"And you hath he quickened, who were dead."* Think about that. We don't like to talk about death, do we? If we knew where we were going to die, we'd probably never go there. If we knew when, we'd try to avoid it. Death is something we don't like to talk about. But why and how do people die? According to verse 1, it is *"in trespasses and sins."* The word "trespass" means "a falling aside when one stood upright," while the word "sins" in this instance refers to missing the mark of God's perfection.

If I were to make a statue, I would probably go look for some marble or clay or wood. I would look for the best materials I could find. But when God came looking for us, He did not come looking for the best. He came looking for those who are dead in trespasses and in sins.

One of the hardest things for people to understand is that we are lost without a savior. Many times if you have wealth or fame or a lot of good things have happened to you, you might look at yourself and say, "I've got it made. I'm OK." But in God's eyes we are dead in trespasses and sins.

We have a number of doctors and nurses in our church. Nowadays doctors can do some amazing things. They can take disfigured faces, for example, and remodel them. They can transplant kidneys. They can replace hearts. I know two pastor friends of mine who have had heart transplants. It's an amazing thing. But one thing a doctor cannot do is raise the dead. In this passage God says that those who were once dead He will make alive.

Verse 2 says, *"Wherein in time past ye walked according to the course of this world, according to the prince of the power of the air, the spirit that now worketh in the children of disobedience."* The spirit of this age holds us in its grip. This verse speaks about the course of the age, which displays a spirit that is hostile to God. Satan is the one who brings evil and influences us to lean on the world like never before. Satan is OK with religion, philosophy, science, culture, education – but Satan does not want you to know God.

Back in this time of the New Testament there was a group called Gnostics, whose name was taken from the Greek word Gnosticism, which refers to the idea of having all knowledge and everything being of the mind. But Paul is saying here, "No, there is a spiritual darkness out here, and we have become the children of the Evil One."

It is interesting how Satan tells you that if you come to Christ you will lose all of your fun and all of your enjoyment. Let me tell you, you don't know what fun is until you become a child of God.

Bob Rodriguez, who went to be with the Lord recently, was the first Spanish-speaking deacon at New Testament Baptist Church. He was always a happy man.

I went to visit him about ten years ago, when I was the new pastor, and his wife was very ill at that time (she did not live long afterward). I remember going into his house and talking to him for an hour; he talked non-stop until I thought it was time to go.

"No, you can't go," he said, and walked into the kitchen. He came out a moment later with a plate of cookies. So we ate all of these cookies and I decided it was time to go.

"No, I've got something else for you," he said before bringing out some kind of Puerto Rican pastry. After we ate that with some milk, he still wouldn't let me go, saying he had some pictures he wanted to show me.

As I was finally leaving, he grabbed me by the lapels and shook me and said, "I just want to remind you that you're my pastor and I'm really going to love you."

"Well, that's great, Bob," I said.

Every time I saw him, even after his wife died and he was lonely, he always tried to tell me a joke. He always tried to say something funny. Don't you think that's a pretty good way to go through life? Bob's joy was always in Christ.

Look at verse 3. *"Among whom also we all had our conversation in times past in the lusts of our flesh, fulfilling the desires of the flesh and of the mind; and were by nature the children of wrath, even as others."* The devil tries to deceive us into thinking that this world is pretty empty unless we seek the desires of the flesh. What this verse is saying is that without God, without hope, without Christ, we really don't have much at all.

So in these first few verses of Ephesians 2, Paul is showing us where we once were, in that valley of despair, before something happened to change our lives. "This is a problem," he seems to be saying.

But I love verse 4, which starts with perhaps the greatest two words in the Bible: *"But God."*

Here was the valley of despair, but God has done something. Sin draws the love of God. We are drawn to things that we like and love, but it was sin that drew the love of God. He said, "I am going to make a way for you."

Look at verses 4-6. *"But God, who is rich in mercy, for his great love wherewith he loved us, Even when we were dead in sins, hath quickened us together with Christ, (by grace ye are saved;) And hath raised us up together, and made us sit together in heavenly places in Christ Jesus."*

Here is what the Bible is saying: Your God is rich.

Now wealth and riches are relative. I can remember a television program called "The $64,000 Question." What does $64,000 really mean today? It may mean a lot to some of us, but not to the wealthy.

We read and hear a lot about millionaires. Back in my childhood, when you talked about a millionaire, you were talking about a lot of money. But there are a lot of people today whose houses are worth a half-million dollars or more, and if they pay them off and have a little money in the bank, they are millionaires. It's simply not as much money as it used to be. Then you consider a billionaire, and his idea of what makes up a lot of money is going to be completely different.

But God is rich. He owns the earth, the universe and all that there is. He owns all that you and I have. And He looks for those who are dead in trespasses and sins.

I read an incredible story recently about a father who had one daughter. The mother had died, and the daughter could not handle life, becoming a hopeless alcoholic. One day her father found her after she had consumed nearly an entire bottle of whiskey. Her face was flushed, she was belligerent and even tried to physically abuse her father until he put his strong arms around her, buckled her up in the car, took her home and put her to bed so he could try to help her become sober. The reporter who told this story said, "That father really loves his daughter."

That's kind of how God looks at us. Because He loves us, he made us alive. He gave us life.

Some of you may have asked Jesus to be your Saviour, yet you don't really feel very alive inside. I think we sometimes don't understand what it is that we are doing. When we come to Christ, it is for one reason – because we were dead in our sin and separated from God.

We don't just get saved to jump up and say, "Now I'm on my way to Heaven," or so we can have our name on a church roll. It's not just so our friends can see us baptized so they'll get off our backs and stop talking to us about Christ. When we get saved, it means that God has given us a brand-new life inside.

If you come to Christ, there are some signs in your life that show how you really have become a child of God, that you are alive in Christ. Take a test and ask yourself, "Am I alive in Christ?"

Look at Acts 2 for a moment. This is a famous passage about Peter's sermon at Pentecost, where more than three thousand came to Christ. Verse 37 says, *"Now when they heard this, they were pricked in their heart, and said unto Peter and to the rest of the apostles, Men and brethren, what shall we do?"* When you come to Christ, there is real conviction. They heard the preaching of the Word of God and were cut to the heart.

Look at verse 38. *"Then Peter said unto them, Repent, and be baptized every one of you in the name of Jesus Christ for the remission of sins, and ye shall receive the gift of the Holy Ghost."* To repent means you were going one way and now you will change your mind and go the opposite way. It means a turning around.

We are not baptized for salvation, but once we're saved we follow the Lord in baptism. There is conviction of sin, and you turn around and say, "There is only one Saviour, and it is the Lord Jesus Christ."

When you get saved, and things happen in your life, you don't need me or someone else to tell you; you realize that there is something different inside. When we go back and do the things we used to do, we think, "I don't know if God is pleased with this." That is conviction of sin.

After they *"gladly received"* Christ in verse 41, the next verse says, *"And they continued stedfastly in the apostles' doctrine and fellowship, and in breaking of bread, and in prayers."* There was an understanding of Scripture, a desire to hear the preaching of the Word of God and to study and discuss the Word of God.

My wife and I have been married more than 40 years and we've really gotten to know each other. Often when she starts talking, I know what she's about to say, and vice versa, because we know and understand each other. When you get saved and start growing in the Lord, you really begin to understand something about God.

Then things don't bug you so much. People don't bug you so much. Problems that come your way aren't nearly as big as you think they are, because God is building your life. It is a sign that you are alive.

In verse 42, the Bible also tells us that there is a bond that you have. The Greek word that is used here for "fellowship" is *koinonia*, which means "a desire to be with the family."

I enjoy working and everything that I do. But when it's time to go home at night, I enjoy going home. I look forward to seeing my home, my cat, my swimming pool, and my study, but I really like seeing my wife.

I have a son who still lives at home, and I love seeing him. If the rest of the family wants to come over, I love seeing them. Why? It's because there is a family bond.

When you become a Christian, there is a tremendous need to be in the world and reach people, but there is also a need for a fellowship with those who understand what this is all about.

Verse 42 also tells us that these early Christians were in prayer. A sign that we are alive is that we pray and we hear God speak to our lives through prayer, through His spirit, and as we begin to pray, God begins to answer our prayers.

In Gal. 4:6 the Bible says that as we begin to understand Him we call Him "Abba Father," which means "Papa Father." All of a sudden we know that we have a new relationship with Him.

Back in Acts 2, verses 46-47 tell us that we have a new heart that God gives to us, for it speaks about praising God and having favor with all the people. There is a desire to please God and be around the people of God.

Also, there is an assurance of salvation that comes into our lives. We know that we are children of God; we sense it deep inside. Nobody can talk you out of it.

Here is another way you know that you are a child of. One of the great signs we find in the book of Ephesians is that once you are saved, you are going to have trouble in your life because the devil doesn't like who you follow.

I have often heard a new Christian say, "Boy, I've got some trouble. I never knew I'd have this much trouble in my life." Friend, when you're a child of God, welcome to trouble.

Today there are more Christian martyrs around the world than at any time in church history. They have died because they took a stand for Christ.

If these are some signs of being alive, let me challenge you to see these signs in your life. Go back to Ephesians 2 and see what God has in store for us, specifically in verses 4 and 7. *"But God, who is rich in mercy, for his great love wherewith he loved us ... That in the ages to come he might shew the exceeding riches of his grace in his kindness toward us through Christ Jesus."*

One recent Wednesday on our church platform we set up tables with awards for some of the outstanding athletic performances of the past year at Dade Christian School. Our football team, for example, was second in the state of Florida in its division for the 2006 season. What a tremendous year. So for this and some of the other teams, we presented plaques and trophies and certificates recognizing these outstanding achievements.

When you go in someone's house and see a trophy, you walk up and see what it represents. For example, a person could get a trophy for bowling a 300 game. "Wow," you say. But you never ask who made the trophy

If you see a beautiful painting in an art gallery, you will likely look to see the signature on the painting because you know someone has painted something powerful.

When God looks at you with His grace – the favor He has given you which you do not deserve – He is saying, "Look at my trophy." But the important thing is not the trophy itself, but the Maker of the trophy. Of us it can be said, "This one belongs to God."

The editor of a magazine recently said, "Storytellers will be the most valued workers of the 21st century." May I say that your story is very important. What is your story? What is your testimony outside of the church?

When God saves us, He transforms our lives. What if we spent one week in prayer seeking God and doing nothing else, asking Him what He wants us to be like?

Author Leonard Sweet said, "What would happen if, for one week, everyone in the United States gave up work, cigarettes, coffee, alcohol, sugar, antidepressants, stimulants, movies, video games and computers?" Some of us wouldn't know what to do. What if we just prayed? There would be a sense of understanding the transformation that happens.

Imagine going to someone who is without God and that person says to you, "I have three months to live. I am going to die." What about your transformed life would help that person? What exactly would you tell him? What is your story?

When I saw that young man wearing a University of Maryland jacket, six-foot-seven with bulging muscles, looking at basketball plays, it wasn't difficult for me to ask, "Are you a basketball player?" There was no doubt what he was about. But as a child of God, what are you about?

When you go to work, you are the transformed person there. At home in your neighborhood, you are the transformed person there. When you are around other people in a public place, you are the transformed person there. The bottom line is this: When God comes into our lives, He makes us alive, so we need to live and act like we are alive.

We don't become perfect, but we do become transformed – a life that has been changed. If you made a decision in Christ that has never changed anything about you, I would suggest to you frankly that you check out your decision.

If you are a Christian, I want to challenge you to live a transformed life. Neighbors, coworkers, and people we come in contact with every day need the Lord. Our lives need to be transformed lives, making a difference in other people's lives.

CHAPTER 4

A ROTTEN APPLE AND A WORK OF ART
Ephesians 2:8-10

—⊙〰⊙—

What if you were on the auction block? How much would someone bid for you? How much would someone bid for your spouse or your children?

There are two instances in the Bible where a word is used that speaks of poetry. One of these words is in the first chapter of Romans, where the Apostle Paul is writing about the creation of the world and refers to the invisible things of God. That passage is saying that God wrote a poem about creation.

The second time is in Eph. 2:8-10. It is found in the word "workmanship." This is a poem God has written about your life. So we have a poem about creation and a poem about redemption. With that in mind, consider the difference between a rotten apple and a work of art.

My wife is not able to do some of the things she used to do because of various physical ailments. As a result, I occasionally do the grocery shopping. My wife and my youngest son, who still lives at home, do a great job at this but I must confess that I do it poorly. She will tell me what to buy, but I'm the kind of person who loads the cart with the first things I find because I'm in a hurry. Even if I don't have to be somewhere else, I'm still in a hurry because I don't want to be in the store very long.

The other day I bought some apples and brought them home. A day or two later I saw them sitting in the bowl and thought, "Those are some beautiful apples." I picked up one and bit into it, and it was rotten on the inside. As I threw it away I thought I'd try a second apple. That one was also rotten.

While I was moaning and groaning about this, my wife said to me, "I told you to check out the apples before you buy them." I told her that I wouldn't know how to check them unless I bit into one in the store.

On the inside, you and I are as rotten as those apples. It's painful to admit it, but we know that it's true. God reminds us of this in the Bible, but He also tells us that we can be works of art.

One of my favorite artists is Thomas Kincade. His paintings are beautiful works of art that make us feel warm and fuzzy inside. God says in Eph. 2:8-10 that we are works of art made by God:

"For by grace are ye saved through faith; and that not of yourselves: it is the gift of God: Not of works, lest any man should boast. For we are his workmanship, created in Christ Jesus unto good works, which God hath before ordained that we should walk in them."

Look at these verses in light of the first verse of the chapter: *"And you hath he quickened, who were dead in trespasses and sins."* There is the rotten apple, and in the later verses we see the work of art. When you accepted Christ, you left the world of rotten apples to be developed into a work of art. You aren't left by the side of road, but you are taken to be made into what God has for you.

To get the total picture of what God has done, go back to verses 4-7. *"But God, who is rich in mercy, for his great love wherewith he loved us, Even when we were dead in sins, hath quickened us together with Christ, (by grace ye are saved;) And hath raised us up together, and made us sit together in heavenly places in Christ Jesus: That in the ages to come he might shew the exceeding riches of his grace in his kindness toward us through Christ Jesus."* Taken as a single passage, verses 4-10 show a union of God's people with Christ. When you come to Christ, you are drawn together with Him in a special union.

We find 93 times in the book of Ephesians the word "*in*" that demonstrates how you, as a believer, are in Christ and He is in you. In fact, the Bible tells us in several places in Ephesians that we are set in heavenly places, as we have already discussed. In the midst of a continual spiritual warfare, you and I who are in Christ have been set apart.

What God has done for us is not mysticism but a living experience. It is new life and new victory. It means that when you come to Christ, there should be a transformation that is taking place in your life. God is doing something in your life that only He can do.

Stop and think about your life. If it is going along just like everyone else's, like those who say they are religious, you need to consider just what God is doing in your life.

There are four key words in this passage that tell us what God did here. The first word is **grace**, found in verses 5 and 8. Both verses state that you are saved by grace. Grace is the objective, the instrument, the cause, the operation that brings us to God. No one comes to God because of anything good that he or she has done, but because of God's unmerited favor toward us.

We may come to church on Sunday all dressed up and thinking that we look pretty good, and we can make it look to each other like we're doing all right, but the fact of the matter is that spiritually, in the eyes of a holy God, we are just a bunch of rotten apples.

Ask yourself, "What is the worst sin anyone could ever commit?" You might say murder, or the abuse of a child, or living in homosexuality, or cheating on your spouse. Normally, when we think about something like this, we look at it in terms of someone else's life and not our own lives. It's always about the other guy.

The first three chapters of Romans outline in a brilliant way how our lives are like rotten apples. In chapter 1 Paul says that the wicked world is lost. In chapter 2 he states that the moral world is lost, and in chapter 3 he just comes right out and says that the entire world is lost without a Saviour.

Look at Rom. 1:27-28. "*And likewise also the men, leaving the natural use of the woman, burned in their lust one toward another; men with men working that which is unseemly, and receiving in themselves that recompence of their error which was meet. And even as they did not like to retain God in their knowledge, God gave them over to a reprobate mind, to do those things which are not convenient; Being filled with all unrighteousness, fornication, wickedness …"*

Since most of us are not fornicators or involved in sexual perversion, we read up to that point with enthusiasm and say, "That's right! Those people are lost." But wait a minute. The very next word is *"covetousness."*

You walk out into the parking lot after church and see a beautiful new Lexus that a 25-year-old man is driving. You're 50 years old and your car will hardly start. You say to yourself, "I'd love to have that car. I wonder how he got it. He must have a rich father." You start to covet.

In Rom. 1:29, covetousness is placed in the same sentence as murder. Look at the rest of that verse: *"… maliciousness; full of envy, murder, debate, deceit, malignity; whisperers."*

You see a couple and you think, "How did he get her to go with him? Boy, he sure married way over his head!" That is the beginning of envy, which God has put in the same category here as murder.

To us, murder and envy are two very different things. Envy can lead to murder, but in our minds murder is much worse. But God puts them in the same sentence, along with strife, deceit and gossip. It is likely that every one of us has spread gossip at some point in our lives. Gossip can even be fun, or so we think. It makes us feel better about ourselves.

Now look at verse 30. *"Backbiters, haters of God, despiteful, proud, boasters, inventors of evil things, disobedient to parents."* You may feel like crawling under the carpet right now.

The final two verses in the chapter complete the list: *"Without understanding, covenantbreakers, without natural affection, implacable, unmerciful: Who knowing the judgment of God, that they which commit such things are worthy of death, not only do the same, but have pleasure in them that do them."* All of these things, some of which we consider extremely vile and others we probably don't give a second thought sometimes, are put here by God in the same paragraph. This shows how the wicked world is lost.

It is interesting how Romans 2 begins, emphasizing how well God knows our hearts. The first verse says, *"Therefore thou art inexcusable, O man, whosoever thou art that judgest: for wherein thou judgest another, thou condemnest thyself; for thou that judgest doest the same things."* We look at the sins in chapter 1 and think how wicked other people are, and how good we are, but God says that if we judge them we are just as bad as they are. Paul wrote this book in the time that the Jewish world and the Gentile world were somewhat segregated, and he is emphasizing the Jewish world in chapter 2 because the Jewish people felt that they were much more religious than the Gentiles. This shows that not only is the wicked world lost, but the moral world is as well.

Beginning in Rom. 1:18 and up to that very familiar passage in Rom. 3:23, Paul talks about how we are rotten apples in the eyes of God. When he says, *"For all have sinned,"* it means that every one of us has missed the mark. It is easy to point out the sin in others, but it's not so easy to do the same in our own lives. It is not just that we sin, but that sin overwhelms us because it is our very nature to be sinners. You can substitute those four words in Rom. 3:23 with, "I have sinned."

This makes every one of us guilty before God. You might say, "I haven't sinned like so-and-so has." It doesn't matter. The wicked world is lost; the moral world is lost; the whole world is lost. That means I am lost and you are lost.

But Rom. 1:24 says, *"Being justified freely by his grace through the redemption that is in Christ Jesus."* Do you see now why we need grace? The grace of God is a free gift that He has given to you and me. You don't earn it or deserve it; there is nothing about you that suggests that you should have it. But God gives it to us in the Person of the Lord Jesus Christ. Without grace, we would amount to nothing in the eyes of a holy God. Thank God for His grace.

The second word I want you to see in Ephesians 2 is **mercy**. Verse 4 says that God is *"rich in mercy."* In this passage mercy represents the outward signs of pity.

In the Old Testament, the Israelites carried the Ark of the Covenant, which contained the mercy seat. The lid had to be removed to represent the removal of sin. It was a picture of God's mercy.

Mercy deals with the heart of God and His love for those who are down and out, which is really all of us. We are under God's wrath, and only God's love, grace and pity can triumph over that. We deserve nothing at God's hand except judgment, but mercy is the act of God giving to us what we do not deserve. God pities us, and as a result He gives us peace.

The third word is **love**. As the latter part of verse 4 shows, it is God's "great love wherewith he loved us." It is the Greek word *agape*, which is unconditional love.

Stop and think about Jesus Christ bleeding on the cross. See Him as they beat and tortured Him, put the crown of thorns on His head. He was beaten across His back. His beard was taken from His face, and the prophet Isaiah said that He was totally beyond recognition. That is what Jesus did for you and me, and there is no love in the world quite like that love.

The fourth word is **kindness**. You see it in verse 7: *"That in the ages to come he might shew the exceeding riches of his grace in his kindness toward us through Christ Jesus."* Here it is a benign word that means sweetness, love and tender action.

Thank God for His grace, mercy, love and kindness. Once you trust in Christ by faith, God will give you faith when you need it. How do we get faith? Rom. 10:17 tells us, *"So then faith cometh by hearing, and hearing by the word of God."*

Saving faith is God's gracious gift. So by God's grace you have been saved by faith, and this holy experience is God's free gift to you.

There is no achievement that gets us to God. There is no religion, no work of philanthropy, no boasting, none of this. We are what we are simply by the love, the kindness, the mercy and the grace of God. That's all we are.

I go out sometimes to Hollywood Park near my south Florida home and take airboat rides. There are peacocks out there. They put their feathers out and strut everywhere. Some of us would like to walk around like that and say, "Look what I've done." But we can't. Verse 9 makes that clear when it says, *"Not of works, lest any man should boast."*

What if I wrote a lie about you and put it on the front page of the Miami Herald? What if it spread across the country? You might say, "I'd get the best lawyer and you'd be history."

Now suppose I lied about you and you responded by putting a brand-new Lexus in my driveway with a message that said, "I love you." I'd probably rethink what I said about you.

Can you imagine what kind of grace God has given to us? From the very beginning, God said that He did not want to deal with anyone's glory but His own. Satan has tried to take the glory away from God over and over again, but the glory belongs only to God.

Our sin is what put Christ on the cross and crucified the blessed Saviour of Heaven. It is our sin that separates us from God. Grace is the attitude that God has with the lawbreaker. Mercy is given to those who are in distress, and our salvation – every single bit of it – is a gift from Almighty God.

Why did God do this? Verse 10 says, *"For we are his workmanship."* The word used in Rom. 1:20 for "creation" is the word we get "poetry" from. The same word is used here for "workmanship." In other words, there was a poem that God wrote for creation, and there is a work of art He is writing concerning our redemption. These passages are speaking about the creative energy and activity of God.

John Calvin put it this way: "This is enough to put away the cackling of such as boast of having any merit, for when they say so they presuppose that they were their own creators." When you were saved, you were saved by God and by God alone.

Now verse 10 says that we should *"walk in"* good works. Good works do not save us, but good works should be performed after we are saved. Contrast this with verse 2, which says, *"Wherein in time past ye walked according to the course of this world."* That's how you walked when you were dead in trespasses and sins, but now that you are saved, it is essential that your good works follow your salvation. The result of being a child of God is a transformed life.

This idea of getting saved just to go to Heaven or for a quick fix of your problems has nothing to do with salvation. Salvation means that our lives are different, that God has resurrected us from death, that we have been created from nothing. You were once a rotten apple, but now God is making of you a work of art. Consider the words of this well-known hymn:

Marvelous grace of our loving Lord
Grace that exceeds our sin and our guilt;
Yonder on Calvary's mount outpoured,
There where the blood of the Lamb was spilled.
Grace, grace, God's grace,
Grace that will pardon and cleanse within.
Grace, grace, God's grace,
Grace that is greater than all our sin.

Like the words of that other great hymn, "Amazing grace, how sweet the sound, that saved a wretch like me." It is the grace of God that saves us.

When He saves you, God also has a purpose for you. No one in the world is a nobody after coming to Christ. You have something you can offer to the work of the Kingdom of God.

Many people followed the events surrounding the death in early 2007 of Anna Nicole Smith, the Marilyn Monroe of her generation. I thought to myself, "Here is this woman, at the age of 39, with all of her millions, and her life is gone." If today were your last day to live, how has the Workman been working on your life? What steps of faith have you been taking?

Go in your mind's eye to a familiar story. One day God came down in His grace and said to a man named Abram, "I want you to go look for a land."

The man said, "I'll go. Where is it?"

"I'm not going to tell you," God said. "Just start looking."

Abram and his family gathered their things and started on their way, not knowing what they were looking for.

Now think about the story of a nation that was in bondage. They had been made slaves because they had become so powerful. While they were in bondage, a redeemer named Moses rose up, and God told him to lead these people out and take them to the promised land.

"I could never do that," Moses said. "I stutter, and I'm a terrible speaker."

"You're the man," God replied. He was doing a work in Moses' life.

A beautiful woman lived in the country of Moab. The Moabites were not believers. One day, because of a famine in the land, a family came to stay in Moab – a father, mother and two grown sons. One of those sons married Ruth. When all three men died, Naomi had to go back to her homeland, a bitter woman. But Ruth told her mother-in-law, "I'll go with you." She agreed to go to what for her was a foreign land and do whatever Naomi asked. God was producing His workmanship in Ruth, and she set out by faith to do what God had for her to do. When you come to Him by faith, you live by faith.

Little did Ruth know that when she got to Bethlehem she would fall in love with a man named Boaz. From that union would come King David and, eventually, the genealogy of our Lord Jesus Christ.

Think about a teenage girl whom no one knew much about, not even her name. But God suddenly came down and said, "You, Mary will give birth to the Messiah." And she did. A lot of people wondered how this was possible. Some would laugh and ridicule her because she was pregnant and not yet married, but this was the Son of God. "I have a work to do in your life," God said to her.

Consider a group of men and women praying behind locked doors. They saw their Saviour crucified and wondered what might happen next to them. But the power of the Holy Spirit came upon them, and they went out and literally changed the world. It was all possible because God was doing a work in their lives.

Wherever you are in life, whatever you are going through, if you trust the Lord, He has a way of working in your life for His purpose, for His honor, and for His glory. It's as if God has a canvas and a brush, and He is painting the picture of your life. No matter what is happening to you right now, God has a purpose for it.

We are saved by grace, not just to go to Heaven, but because God has a plan to produce a special workmanship in your life. Let Him do the work He wants to do.

CHAPTER 5

NO MORE PREJUDICE
Ephesians 2:11-22

—⟨⟩⟨⟩—

If you are a parent and have more than one child, you have probably told them on many occasions, "You two need to get along." It's even harder when you say that to two adults. But we often find ourselves, in the business world and all facets of society, just trying to get people to get along with each other. It's not the easiest thing.

All of us are familiar with prejudice. Many times people say that Christians are intolerant people. But the fact of the matter is that Christians are probably the most tolerant, because when you think about it, every person who wants to be part of the body of Christ can be.

Yet the story of human history is filled with examples of prejudice and how we treat each other and show partiality to certain people or groups of people.

Years ago I was preaching in a certain town at a conference, and while I was there one day I decided to take a walk through the town. This was back when places like Sam's Club and Costco were first established around the country. So as I was walking, I saw this large store and thought I'd like to see what was inside. I didn't know that it was one of these clubs.

I went up to the front door and a man stood there wearing a uniform. You could tell that he really liked his uniform because he spoke with a great deal of authority.

"Do you have a membership card?" he asked.

"No," I replied.

"Out!"

I turned around and left in a hurry. I couldn't go in because it was a private club.

We understand that certain clubs require certain cards to enter, but everyone is welcome within the body of Christ. In our nation we have seen battles between blacks and whites, Indians and Anglos, men and women, rich and poor. Sometimes a man will have a bad experience with a woman and decide that all women are bad, or vice versa. We have even seen struggles between strong Christians and weak ones.

There are all kinds of prejudices we could talk about. In Paul's day, when he was writing the book of Ephesians, there was a strong prejudice as well.

The gift that God gave the Jewish people during Old Testament times was the gift of the Scriptures. The promise of the Messiah was going to come through the Jews, and the Gentiles knew this. So there was prejudice between the Jew and the Gentile. This is perhaps the biggest struggle with prejudice in human history. It is still going on today and could eventually trigger a great world war.

In the Old Testament, when God began to work through a group of people, He would often give them a symbol. For instance, after the Flood, God placed a rainbow in the sky and told Noah, "I will never again destroy the world with a flood." From my home in south Florida you can see many beautiful rainbows, and they are constant reminders of God's promise to us.

Another symbol going back to the time of Abraham was the practice of circumcision. This was a very important part of the law in the Old Testament.

Today we have the ordinance of baptism, which we urge every person to take part in after trusting Christ. This is a symbol in your life and mine that you are following the Lord.

In the second chapter of Ephesians, Jews and Gentiles are described in a very unique way. Verse 11 says, *"Wherefore remember, that ye being in time past Gentiles in the flesh, who are called Uncircumcision by that which is called the Circumcision in the flesh made by hands."*

Gentiles were referred to as being uncircumcised, and if you were not a Jew at this time you were considered a Gentile. These terms were not used in a kind fashion between these races or cultures in Paul's day, but rather forcefully – almost as a slur. What Paul is saying in this verse is that there is no circumcision or uncircumcision in the body of Christ.

If you know Christ as your Saviour, you understand that we came into this body of believers in somewhat different ways but all of us came by way of the gospel. We all came because of what Jesus Christ has done for us. Even though we don't all know each other personally – you may not even know every member of your own church – we as believers around the world are all part of the body of Christ, and every one of us is special and unique within that body. There is to be no prejudice at all in that.

My mother and father had two children who died in infancy. I also had an older brother and sister who moved out on their own when my other sister and I were quite young. I was very close to the sister I was raised with, and while I loved my older siblings just as much, I didn't know them as well because they had moved on. But they were still part of my family.

In much the same way, we are all part of the family of God. Each one of us is His workmanship, His poetry, His work of art, and we are all very special in His eyes. So there should be no prejudice about anything in our lives between brothers and sisters in the family of God. We were all once outside that family, whether we were Jew or Gentile, and we all came together only because of the Lord Jesus Christ.

With that in mind, notice the progression in these verses, beginning with us in our natural state. Look at verses 11-12. *"Wherefore remember, that ye being in time past Gentiles in the flesh, who are called Uncircumcision by that which is called the Circumcision in the flesh made by hands; That at that time ye were without Christ, being aliens from the commonwealth of Israel, and strangers from the covenants of promise, having no hope, and without God in the world."*

We have already seen in Ephesians the word "dispensation." A dispensation is a period of time during which God deals in a unique way with a group of people.

In the Old Testament God dealt with Abraham. Circumcision was the sign of the special relationship God had with the Israelites. Today God does not use any signs such as rainbows or circumcision. He uses a new sign that shows we are in the body of Christ.

Eph, 1:12 says, *"That we should be to the praise of his glory, who first trusted in Christ. In whom ye also trusted, after that ye heard the word of truth, the gospel of your salvation: in whom also after that ye believed, ye were sealed with that holy Spirit of promise."*

The Gentiles who looked at the Jews of this day wanted what they had. The word *"commonwealth"* in Eph. 2:12 is a political term that shows how the Gentiles wanted what the Jews had, but they did not know how to go after it.

If you look at pictures of people as they worshipped back in this time, whether they be Greek or Roman or Egyptian, you will find that many people had images and idols of beasts and people lusting and warring, yet everyone is somehow searching for God. The Gentiles looked at the Jewish religion and said, "Yes, there is hypocrisy and pride there, but they have the Scriptures, and there is something about that we want to have."

In the Old Testament there is a marvelous story about Elimelech, his wife Naomi, and their sons Mahlon and Chilion. (Aren't those great names for boys?) There was a famine in Bethlehem, so Elimelech took his family and settled in Moab, which was a land that had false gods everywhere. Little did they know that a crisis would hit them once they got there.

Mahlon and Chilion married two beautiful women of Moab, Orpah and Ruth. Then Elimelech and his two sons died. Because of this, Naomi becomes a very bitter person. She has lost her sons and her husband, so she is going back to the land of Bethlehem, her homeland.

When she makes the announcement to Ruth and Orpah, they both say that they will go with her because they love her. "No," says Naomi. "You stay here." Orpah decides to stay, but Ruth insists on accompanying Naomi back to her home.

So many times in a wedding ceremony, we hear those beautiful words, "Wherever you go, I will go; wherever you lodge, I will lodge; your people will be my people, and your God will be my God." Those words that so many husbands and wives have said to each other were originally the words of Ruth to Naomi.

It seems that Ruth was giving up her entire life to go with Naomi, but the real reason for this decision is that Ruth wanted Naomi's God. Gentiles in the Old Testament age could be a part of the family of God just like they could in the New Testament. Also, just being a Jew did not automatically get a person into God's family in the Old or New Testament. But it becomes clear in the New Testament that Jews and Gentiles must come together.

Look in verse 12 at four phrases that really describe the prejudice that can surface if we're not careful. *"That at that time ye were without Christ"* means you were separated from Christ. *"Being aliens from the commonwealth of Israel"* means you had no rights of citizenship. Then the verse says, *"Strangers from the covenants of promise"* and *"having no hope."*

May I suggest that there are no sadder words in the English language than the two words "no hope." You go to the doctor and he says, "There is no hope." You hear at the scene of a disaster or an accident, "There is no hope." What this verse is saying is that there is no hope in our natural state because we are strangers from the covenant of God.

Go back to the first part of this chapter. It starts out by talking about our sinful condition, and then in verse 4 we see those beautiful words, "But God." Aren't you glad that God enters into all of this? We see something similar in verse 13, which begins, "But now in Christ Jesus." There is hope because we go from our natural state into our new state, away with the old and in with the new.

Now read the entire verse. "But now in Christ Jesus ye who sometimes were far off are made nigh by the blood of Christ." Jesus is the Messiah, the Saviour of all, the meeting point for every single one of us. Jesus takes the Jew and the Gentile and draws us together so that we are brothers and sisters in Christ.

Several years ago I was preaching some meetings in India with several pastors, and we went over to a place called Mud Island. I will never forget that the rest of my life. It was a literal island surrounded by muddy water that contained everything imaginable. I will not even begin to describe the condition of that water, which we had to cross in a small boat.

There was a little pier, with no handles to hold onto on your way to the boat. As I walked across the pier, I prayed, "Dear God, please don't let me fall into this water." I stumbled once and then literally leaped into the boat; I didn't think I could jump that far, but I did what I had to do to avoid falling into that filthy water.

We went out to this island for evening services. People would flock to the service from everywhere. Many of them were Hindus. They would stare at us, seemingly without blinking, as we preached. Scores of them each night would come to Christ.

Many came wanting to accept Jesus along with the other gods they already had. We would have to explain to them that Jesus was not just one god, but He was the only God and you must come to Him alone. With some of them, you could tell that it suddenly clicked. They were no longer far off, but were being drawn nigh.

The term "far off" in Ephesians is a very interesting one, based on a Hebrew expression. Jerusalem was considered the Holy City, and the farther you were from Jerusalem, the farther you would be from the presence of God. Here it is being used to demonstrate that the farther you are from Jesus, the farther you are from God.

Look at verses 14-15. *"For he is our peace, who hath made both one, and hath broken down the middle wall of partition between us; Having abolished in his flesh the enmity, even the law of commandments contained in ordinances; for to make in himself of twain one new man, so making peace."* Jesus is the only way that Jew and Gentile can come together, because He is the One who breaks down that middle wall.

What kind of wall is this? In the temple area, there was a strong palisade that was four and a half feet high. Gentiles could walk in that area but could go no farther; in fact, they could be arrested and imprisoned, perhaps put to death, if they did.

Paul was an interesting person. Wherever he went, either revival or a riot broke out. Acts 21:26 says, *"Then Paul took the men, and the next day purifying himself with them entered into the temple, to signify the accomplishment of the days of purification, until that an offering should be offered for every one of them."* He was saying, "Jesus died and rose again, so we don't need the sacrifices anymore."

According to the next two verses, *"And when the seven days were almost ended, the Jews which were of Asia, when they saw him in the temple, stirred up all the people, and laid hands on him, Crying out, Men of Israel, help: This is the man, that teacheth all men every where against the people, and the law, and this place: and further brought Greeks also into the temple, and hath polluted this holy place."*

Imagine the Apostle Paul walking into the temple, saying, "Come on in, ladies and gentlemen. It's OK. Since Jesus died and rose again, this is not the same holy place anymore." This makes the Jewish leaders want to grab him. The middle wall between Jew and Gentile has come down.

When you and I come to Christ, whether you are a wealthy person or a homeless one, we all come to Him the exact same way. There is no difference. When two people come forward in a church service to accept Christ, one in an expensive suit of clothes and the other wearing the only suit he owns, both come to Christ just as they are.

It's not Jew or Gentile, or any other division, because God has broken all of those down. It's out with the old and in with the new.

Eph. 2:16 says, *"And that he might reconcile both unto God in one body by the cross, having slain the enmity thereby."* To reconcile means to restore or put back together. I believe in counseling for people who have problems, marital or otherwise, but any counseling that does not have a foundation in Jesus Christ will go nowhere.

Paul is making that clear in this passage, saying in verses 17-18, *"And came and preached peace to you which were afar off, and to them that were nigh. For through him we both have access by one Spirit unto the Father."* The word *"access"* here is the Greek word from which we get the word "passage." It was actually a title that was given to an official of an Oriental court, so that if you wanted to go and visit a king, you had to go by way of the access, or the man who could bring you in there. There is only one way to God, and that access is in the Person of our Saviour.

John Phillips, in one of his commentaries, tells a story about Buckingham Palace and a little boy who often stood outside the gate wishing he could go in. But he never could.

One day a man came walking by and saw that boy standing there. He took the boy's hand and said, "Come with me." They walked right through the palace to where the king was.

When the man saw the king, he said, "Hello, Father." That little boy had been brought into the palace by the king's son.

That is exactly how we have access to our Heavenly Father, and you have access to your salvation. It is how we have access to Heaven and to purpose in our lives – through the Person of Jesus Christ.

All of America needs this message. We need to go and tell our friends and do everything we can to help them understand that Jesus Christ is the only access to having purpose and meaning in life.

Our next step is to go from our natural state to a new state to a new family. Look at verse 19. *"Now therefore ye are no more strangers and foreigners, but fellow citizens with the saints, and of the household of God."*

We have had special services in our church with important Israeli leaders in business and government, and we invited the unsaved Jewish community in south Florida to come because we want the Jewish people in this area to know that there is a church that loves them so we can reach them with the gospel. Whether you are Spanish, or Italian, or African, you need to get the gospel to your people and give them the glorious message that Jesus saves.

"Fellow citizens" is a political term here that referred to someone who belonged to a brand-new country. The Old Testament privileges that you derived from being born into a Jewish family still had great meaning, but they had no meaning when it came to getting into the Kingdom of God, because the only way there is through Jesus Christ.

You may have a last name that you know has some kind of meaning to you. This is true in many cultures. My last name is Pedrone, pronounced "Pe-DRONE." Originally it was Pedone, pronounced

"Pe-DOUGH-nay." If you ever visit Italy and go to Rome, you will see "Pedone" signs everywhere; it means "pedestrian."

My uncle Tony, when he came to America at the beginning of the 20th century, knew what he was doing. By adding that "r" to his last name, it became "boss" or "landowner." I like that.

In a Jewish family, the last name had great significance. But the Bible says here that it is not your last name that is important, but your relationship to Christ.

Notice how the last three verses in this chapter speak about a new habitation. *"And are built upon the foundation of the apostles and prophets, Jesus Christ himself being the chief corner stone; In whom all the building fitly framed together groweth unto an holy temple in the Lord: In whom ye also are builded together for an habitation of God through the Spirit.*

The Jews loved their rabbinical traditions. The Gentiles loved their philosophies. These verses are saying that neither of those are important. The Old Testament God is the New Testament God, and the Old Testament temple gives way to the saving work of Jesus Christ.

Ephesians 3 talks about mystery. Paul is referring to something that God has never told you about so clearly before. That mystery, mentioned in verse 2, is the grace of God. It is mentioned several more times in that chapter and again in chapter 4. It is the wonderful understanding that you and I go into God's Kingdom, not for having Jewish tradition or Gentile philosophies, but because of the Lord Jesus Christ.

When I was a young pastor in Pennsylvania, I was involved with an organization that concerned itself with the morality of our city and eventually became the state director of that organization, which allowed me to meet with various state leaders. I will never forget how, as a young man in my late 20s, I was invited to have breakfast at the Governor's Mansion in Harrisburg, Penn. The governor at that time was Richard Thornburg.

When I went in, it was just the governor and his wife, another man and me. We had a great time. Both he and his wife said that they were believers. As I left the Governor's Mansion I felt as if I had met with royalty. As I drove back to my home town I got further and further away.

That's how people felt when they left Jerusalem in New Testament times. They would go into the temple and sense the presence of God. Then they would go back to their homes and feel like they were so far away from that presence. That all changed one day when the Saviour was born.

When you go to Jerusalem today, you still can sense something special and new. But you don't have to go to Jerusalem, or to the Governor's Mansion, to feel the presence of royalty. You are already royalty in Christ. We don't deserve it; it's all because of grace. But we are royalty if we have Christ in our lives.

The same Person who lives with you when you are at church lives with you at home or wherever you are. He lives within you when you go to bed at night and when you get up in the morning. He is the Holy Spirit. He has sealed you, and you are a royal member of the family of God. So you should live like it.

Your economic status or your culture means nothing here, because in the family of God there is absolutely no prejudice.

The Gentiles in Ephesus were saying, "We like your scriptures." The Jews replied, "All right. Get circumcised." Even today, to convert to Judaism a male must be circumcised. There are rites and traditions that must be observed, just as they were back then. The Jews had the same curiosity about Gentile traditions.

But Paul said, "Wait a minute. It's neither Jew nor Gentile, but an old rugged cross and empty tomb." When you see that, you can come away as a member of the royal family of God.

Vince Lombardi was one of the greatest football coaches in history. The Super Bowl trophy is named after him. When he went to the Green Bay Packers, they were the worst team in professional football, but within a year they had become respectable.

One of his players, Jerry Kramer, came in one day weeping, saying, "Thank you, coach, for making us respectable. Our kids can go to school now and not be laughed at."

A few years later, the Packers were the champions of the NFL. Lombardi told his players, "You are champions on the field. You need to live like champions off the field – humble and thankful for what you have."

As children of God, we need to live like we belong to the King of Kings. It's a special position to be in.

CHAPTER 6

GOD'S NEW SOCIETY
Ephesians 3:1-13

I have three questions for you to consider.

First question: What was your favorite subject in school? You might say that history was your favorite. History is often what we make it.

In 1919, Henry Ford was involved in a lawsuit with the Chicago Tribune, and they began discussing the automobile he had developed and whether it had any value. As they discussed the way people traveled at various times in history, Ford said from the witness stand, "History is nothing but bunk." He said that because it wasn't helping him prove his point.

Karl Marx wrote, "History is really dialectical." What he meant was that if you asked a lot of questions, you could make history mean whatever you wanted. He accomplished that with communism.

Some history is just the memorization of rote facts, like dates, kings, wars, generals, and important people. Many who have only memorized certain facts might ask, "What is the point of history?"

Christianity teaches us that history is really "His story." It is the story of God. The Bible connects the war between good and evil and tells us that Christ has won a decisive victory over sin.

Second question: What is a mystery? A mystery contains episodes about something that is unknown, unexplained, a secret that is kept, and that keeps people interested. We want to unravel the unexplained, and solve the mystery.

The third chapter of Ephesians tells us about a great mystery.

Third question: What church were you raised in? Maybe it was a Lutheran, or Presbyterian, or Catholic, or Methodist, or Baptist, or some other denomination or type of church. Perhaps you didn't go to church when you were young. Looking back on this makes us think of many different things.

So with these questions on the table, think about the three key words – history, mystery, and church.

Look at Eph. 3:1-13. *"For this cause I Paul, the prisoner of Jesus Christ for you Gentiles, If ye have heard of the dispensation of the grace of God which is given me to you-ward: How that by revelation he made known unto me the mystery; (as I wrote afore in few words, Whereby, when ye read, ye may understand my knowledge in the mystery of Christ) Which in other ages was not made known unto the sons of men, as it is now revealed unto his holy apostles and prophets by the Spirit; That the Gentiles should be fellow heirs, and of the same body, and partakers of his promise in Christ by the gospel: Whereof I was made a minister, according to the gift of the grace of God given unto me by the effectual working of his power. Unto me, who am less than the least of all saints, is this grace given, that I should preach among the Gentiles the unsearchable riches of Christ; And to make all men see what is the fellowship of the mystery, which from the beginning of the world hath been hid in God, who created all things by Jesus Christ: To the intent that now unto the principalities and powers in heavenly places might be known by the church the manifold wisdom of God, According to the eternal purpose which he purposed in Christ Jesus our Lord: In whom we have boldness and access with confidence by the faith of him. Wherefore I desire that ye faint not at my tribulations for you, which is your glory."*

Paul was writing these words from jail, where he was a prisoner of Nero because of his stand for the cause of Christ. He mentions his tough times in that last verse, but says not to worry about his tribulations, because he is a prisoner for the sake of the Gentiles.

There are 80 or more different people groups in my church in south Florida on a typical Sunday morning. We have people from everywhere. But in the book of Ephesians, Paul breaks it down to just two – the Jew and the Gentile. The Old Testament scriptures were given to the Jewish people, although Jews and Gentiles could be saved. Ruth, from Moab, is an example of that. But in the New Testament, God introduces a brand-new society.

Paul writes here that he has received a certain revelation, meaning that God has given it to him, and that a commission has also been given to him, which he must then give to you. He calls it a mystery.

So we should consider two things. What is the mystery? What is the ministry?

A mystery is something dark, obscure or secretive. It is something that cannot be explained. Years ago, the infamous labor leader (some say Mafia leader) Jimmy Hoffa disappeared. He is presumed dead, but no one knew where his body was. Some people believe that he is buried beneath the end zone at Giants Stadium in East Rutherford, New Jersey. There has been talk of digging up the field to see if his body is really there. That is a mystery.

After the starlet Anna Nicole Smith died in early 2007, everyone was asking how she died and initially no one was certain. It was a mystery.

The Bible speaks several times about a mystery in this passage, and it is the Greek word *mysterion*, which means something that is not necessarily a closely guarded secret. It is different than what you and might think of as a mystery.

Back in New Testament times, people would often speak about a mystery, and it was the idea of a religion that had initiation rites that people would follow to become a member. But in Christianity there is no esoteric mystery for the elite, because the mystery here is spoken of by God, and in verses 4-6 of this chapter we are told what the mystery is.

What is the best way to unite people? Some say it is through government and politics, or through the family, or something else. This passage is saying that the best way to draw people together is through the revelation of what God has done, or this great mystery: God has called Jews and Gentiles to be co-heirs, and share the promises of God, and have the same blessings of God. The mystery of Christ is the complete union of Jew and Gentile with Him and in Him.

It doesn't matter what people group you come from, where you have lived, or what your economic status might be. We can all be blended together in what is called the family of God, through the Person of the Lord Jesus Christ.

When we gather at church for a Sunday service, we are not gathering as an Old Testament people or a New Testament people. Under the old theocracy of the Jewish nation, it was taught that God's work would one day be terminated and replaced by a new society. That new society is here, and it is founded in Christ.

Have you ever heard people say that Christianity is really intolerant? That is absolutely wrong. There is nothing as tolerant as Christianity. When you understand who Jesus is – that He died, was buried and rose again, and He is God the Son – you realize that everyone is welcome in the family of God.

You might say, "But you don't know what my past is like, where I've been and what I've done." Let me assure you that it does not matter, because when you come to the Cross and to the Saviour, the mystery is revealed that God brings everyone into His family the same way. Whether you are a child, a parent or a grandparent, whatever your circumstances, everyone needs to know Jesus Christ.

I don't mean just making a profession of faith and saying, "Now I'm on my way to Heaven." There needs to be a passion in our lives that makes us say, "I love Christ and want Him to be first in my life." I want to challenge you to do that in your own life. The heart of our ministry must be the lordship of Jesus Christ.

So Paul not only writes about the mystery, which is the Jew and Gentile becoming one, but also the ministry that he wanted to make known. This begins in verse 7:

"Whereof I was made a minister, according to the gift of the grace of God given unto me by the effectual working of his power. Unto me, who am less than the least of all saints, is this grace given, that I should preach among the Gentiles the unsearchable riches of Christ."

The proper translation of the first part of verse 8 is "the leastest of the least." It sounds like something our kindergarten children might come home and say. But he's not speaking about a linguistic issue. It's a theological issue. He is saying, "I realize what I am and who I am in Christ," and he talks about his ministry beyond that.

God wants to see you saved, but He also has a purpose for your life. God has a reason for you to be living on this earth. We're not here just to make money or have good times together and then die one day. We're here for a reason.

Not long ago I visited a family that had a sudden death in the home. The mother asked me, "Is this all that life is about? Do you just eat, work, have a little fun, and then it's over? It that all there is?"

One Saturday night as we were preparing for the services the next day, we learned that the husband of one of our Christian school teachers, a man in his 40s, died suddenly in the Florida Keys. We were immediately reminded of how quickly life comes and goes.

Life does not come just so we can say, "I have lived a life." Your life and mine need to have a purpose. Paul wrote in these verses about his purpose, first by saying that he is to make Christ and His riches known to the Gentiles.

Throughout the first two chapters of Ephesians, Paul talks about a number of things, including our resurrection from the death of sin; victorious enthronement with Christ reconciliation with God; incorporation into a new society; the end of hostility and beginning of peace; access to God through Christ; and membership in God's family.

In these verses in Ephesians 3, Paul uses the word *unsearchable*. It means inexhaustible or infinite. It means that if the gospel is true, then it needs to be received and it needs to be told.

A good Bible-believing church should be a place where people feel at home. Someone might say, "But I'm not a Christian. I only come to church a couple of times a year." Our attitude to that person should be: "I hope you feel at home with us. The family of God is a place where you should feel welcome to enter. And we have something you need – a Saviour who gives purpose in life."

Paul wanted everyone to know the riches that are in Christ. Our goal as Christians should be that the lost world know those riches and joy we have in Christ. God does so many wonderful things, even though sometimes we don't know exactly how He is working. But we should be thankful for the wonderful privileges God gives us.

I am a grandfather, but when I see a children's program at church I think back to when my wife and I had small children. We were married nine years without children and came to believe that we would not be able to have any. We got a group of people together to pray for us, and our first child came along soon after that. Before we knew it, we had four beautiful children. I thought I should tell those people to stop praying.

Do you know what is really important in your life? One of the most important things is to make sure your child loves Jesus. What is in your life that makes your child or grandchild love Him?

The Bible says in 2 Cor. 4:6, "For God, who commanded the light to shine out of darkness, hath shined in our hearts, to give the light of the knowledge of the glory of God in the face of Jesus Christ." We are to be giving out the light. In this society that God has ordained, He includes all who come unto Him in mutual reconciliation to be part of the great family of God.

Paul also says that we need to make God's wisdom known to the cosmic powers. In the church of Jesus Christ, there is multi-racial, multi-cultural community. We are from all over the world. What binds us together in a lasting way? It is our relationship to God in this mystery of the great society He has brought together.

With all of this in mind, Paul writes about the gospel being spread throughout the world, as well as the idea of rulers and authorities, and living in a time of real spiritual warfare. But he gives four thoughts that I believe are very important.

First is the centrality of the church and the fact that the church is all about relationship. Christianity is not just a religion, but above everything else it is a personal relationship with Jesus Christ. Being a member of a church and baptized in water, having a certain type of church background – none of that means anything if there is not first a relationship with Christ.

Verse 11 says, *"According to the eternal purpose which he purposed in Christ Jesus our Lord."* God has purpose for your life, and the centrality of the church shows that we are in a relationship with Him as well as with one another.

Next, consider the centrality of the church to history. As I stated earlier, history is often what we make it, but it is really the story of God and the affairs of people. Nothing happens by chance with God. He knows everything about anything that is taking place. God is in charge of it all.

Then there is the centrality of the church to the gospel. There is really no other message that we need than the gospel – that Jesus died, was buried and rose again, and we come to Him by realizing that we cannot save ourselves, but by repenting of our sins and trusting Him by faith.

Finally, there is the centrality of the church to Christian living. Look at the words of Jesus in Matt. 25:31-40.

"When the Son of man shall come in his glory, and all the holy angels with him, then shall he sit upon the throne of his glory: And before him shall be gathered all nations: and he shall separate them one from another, as a shepherd divideth his sheep from the goats: And he shall set the sheep on his right hand, but the goats on the left. Then shall the King say unto them on his right hand, Come, ye blessed of my Father, inherit the kingdom prepared for you from the foundation of the world: For I was an hungred, and ye gave me meat: I was thirsty, and ye gave me drink: I was a stranger, and ye took me in: Naked, and ye clothed me: I was sick, and ye visited me: I was in prison, and ye came unto me. Then shall the righteous answer him, saying, Lord, when saw we thee an hungred, and fed thee? or thirsty, and gave thee drink? When saw we thee a stranger, and took thee in? or naked, and clothed thee? Or when saw we thee sick, or in prison, and came unto thee? And the King shall answer and say unto them, Verily I say unto you, Inasmuch as ye have done it unto one of the least of these my brethren, ye have done it unto me."

When you come to Christ, He gives you purpose in life. The message for us from Ephesians is that God has raised up a new society, and our investment is not just to be in ourselves or our families, but in all of the people we come in contact with. It's not just about saying you're a member of a church, but literally being the Jesus that He would want us to be.

Many of us work many hours to help people and minister in our communities because we feel that we are doing what Jesus said we should do. But that is not a job for a few elite. It is for everyone in this grand new society to do what God would have us do. If you know Christ as your Saviour, you need to examine just how you are operating in God's society.

CHAPTER 7

WHAT IS THE REASON?
Ephesians 3:14-21

_____ༀ_____

In verses 1 and 14 of Ephesians 3, the first three words are the same: *"For this cause."* Another way of saying it could be "for this reason," as the Apostle Paul is answering some "why" questions in this chapter.

Look at verse 14. *"For this cause I bow my knees unto the Father of our Lord Jesus Christ."* Paul is not just literally bowing his knees here, but he is bowing himself to the will of his Lord and Saviour.

A number of years ago I was on my second trip to the Holy Land. On those trips we usually had a day off in the middle, and we would go into old Jerusalem to shop and see the sights. I was there this time with some friends when a group of police officers suddenly came running through the old city.

I asked people what was going on, and they said there was something happening at the Temple Mount, which you could visit freely at that time (now you need permission to go there). It wasn't the smartest thing to do, but since I was young and full of energy I decided I would go find out what was going on. Only one other man in my group wanted to go with me, so off we went to the Temple Mount.

When we got there, I asked a guard what was going on. He said that there were five Jewish university students who had gone in and were trying to take over the Temple Mount, which was run by

Muslims. They had quickly been apprehended and were already in jail as I was speaking to this guard.

As I went up into the Temple Mount, I saw an astonishing sight. There were thousands of Muslims facing Mecca and praying, and you could hear a pin drop. The guard would not tell me what they were praying about, and I realized that as a young man from the United States who looked very American, perhaps the best thing for me to do was get out of there.

I thought about that throng of people on their knees in prayer, and I considered how sincere they must have been to come and pray like that, no matter whom they were praying to or what their prayers were about.

You and I are so privileged to have an opportunity for a relationship with the God of Heaven, and sometimes we just don't take advantage of it like we should.

Verse 15 says, *"Of whom the whole family in heaven and earth is named."* It was court etiquette in this day that you would bow whenever you approached someone special. The Bible says that we can come boldly to God anytime we want, because He loves us and wants to hear from us. But let me remind you today that He is still God, and He deserves the greatest respect and dignity when we go to Him.

The Greek word in verse 14 for *"Father"* is *Pater*, and it refers to "the one and only true Father of all." In verse 15 the word for *"family"* is *patria*, taken from the same root word, and these verses are saying that all fatherhood is derived from God the Father, who is the Father of Fathers and the pattern of fatherhood.

Sigmund Freud once taught that we invented God because we needed a father figure. But Paul is saying here, "I bow to the Father in Heaven; He is the source of all conceivable fatherhood."

I find it very interesting every year when Father's Day is approaching, as I search for poetry and other nice words to fit this occasion, that there is very little written about fathers. There is a great deal written about mothers, almost to the point of sainthood. But when we look for a role model for fathers, the best example we have is the fatherhood of God.

When Jesus taught us to pray, He said in Matt. 6:9, *"Our Father which art in heaven, Hallowed be thy name."* I don't think any of our children come up to us as fathers and call us "hallowed." But when we talk about the God of Heaven, it is a holy reverence that He deserves, and it is a privilege that we can go straight to Him in prayer.

By beginning this passage with *"for this cause,"* Paul is showing us the reason why he is bowing before God. These verses demonstrate the power of God and the petition of God.

The power of God is seen in verse 16. *"That he would grant you, according to the riches of his glory, to be strengthened with might by his Spirit in the inner man."* A wealthy person may give a trifling amount of his riches, but it might not be proportionate to what he can actually give. God is not giving "out of" His riches, but *"according to"* His riches.

Napoleon once gave a great amount of wealth to a man, and he was asked why. "Because he honored me by the magnitude of his request," Napoleon replied.

A poet once wrote, "You are coming to a king, large petitions with you bring, for his grace and power are such, none can ever ask too much."

With that in mind, let me ask you this: When you go before God, what big thing are you asking of Him? Maybe you ask for something big but believe He is not going to give it because you're not supposed to be asking for it.

Psalm 37:4 says, *"Delight thyself also in the LORD: and he shall give thee the desires of thine heart."* He will even give you those things you want to ask Him for but think they are too big. Ephesians 3 is saying that we have a right of access to God according to His riches, and He is pretty rich, isn't He?

The second half of verse 16 talks about petitioning God to be strengthened by His Spirit. Prov. 20:27 says, *"The spirit of man is the candle of the LORD."* So what governs us? Sometimes it is instinct, intellect, or emotions. Occasionally it is our will or conscience. All of these things can lead you astray. But here we find that it should be the directing influence of the Holy Spirit of God that leads us.

When we accept Christ, the Holy Spirit reigns in our lives and it is our responsibility to submit to the lordship of Christ by submitting to the work of the Holy Spirit. We should constantly be saying, "God, what are you saying to me?"

That leads us into the next petition, in verse 17: *"That Christ may dwell in your hearts by faith; that ye, being rooted and grounded in love."* What an amazing thought He is giving us here.

Jesus Christ ministered on Earth for about three years. He walked, talked, laughed, worked, knew pain and pleasure, was tempted, knew the pressures of life – He was God but also man. In this passage, we see the idea that Christ should abide and make His permanent home in our hearts. His home is in Heaven, but also in our hearts. Is Jesus at home in your heart?

Recently I had a busy week with some travel in addition to church responsibilities, so on a Tuesday afternoon I called my wife to tell her that I would be staying at my office late to study and prepare for Wednesday and Sunday services. My wife, to whom I have been married more than 40 years, said, "I'll miss you. Come home as soon as you can." Needless to say, that was enough to at least make me reconsider my plans. I decided to work extra hard so I could get home sooner.

What is home? For me, it is a nice house on a lake with a pool. It has all of my stuff, like my television and stereo and other recreational devices. There is even a cat. But most of all, my wife is there, so I want to be there.

Jesus wants us to have that kind of attitude when we welcome Him into our hearts. Just as He lived His earthly life in the power of the Spirit, in communion and cooperation with the Father, we are to live in communion and cooperation with Him.

Look at Col. 1:27. *"To whom God would make known what is the riches of the glory of this mystery among the Gentiles; which is Christ in you, the hope of glory."* The genius of the gospel is that it is about Christ, and Christianity is about Christ. Religion is about religion, but Christianity is the living Christ taking up His residence in our hearts and lives, and when we apply the faith principle by grace, we must believe that His indwelling in us is a fact and turn the control of our lives over to Him. His life, not ours, produces the

Christian conduct, conversation and citizenship that we need to have in our lives.

The last part of verse 17 talks about *"being rooted* [biological term] *and grounded* [construction term] *in love."* When I met my wife years ago and we started talking about marriage, it was because we wanted to live together the rest of our lives. This verse talks about living with Christ in you, and love making up the basis for your life.

Love is the soil of the soul. The essential nutrient is the fragrance of Christianity. It is God's everlasting love which Jesus exhibited on the cross. The word used for *"grounded"* refers to the foundation of a building, the same word used by Jesus when he talked about whether to build our house on sand or a rock.

The fact that God loves us is pretty overwhelming, isn't it? A great theologian traveled around the world preaching, and when he came home he was asked by a newspaper reporter, "What is the greatest truth you know?"

"Only this," he replied. "Jesus loves me, this I know, for the Bible tells me so."

When Christ comes to live within us, there is a root and a ground of love that God gives to us. He examines it this way in verse 18: *"May be able to comprehend with all saints what is the breadth, and length, and depth, and height."*

If you want the length of something, you draw a line. If you add breadth, you have a surface area. If you add depth, you have a solid. But how do you measure height?

I am five feet, eight inches tall. I might want to be six-feet-eight but I can't be. You can sometimes lose height but as an adult you can't add height. How does God add height in this case?

When the Bible talks about Heaven, it mentions length, breadth and depth, but not height. John Phillips said that God's love is absolutely without comprehension. Think about how long His love is. When did God start loving you? Was it when He first saw you, or when you were born? No, He has loved you forever. Even the most despicable person you can imagine is loved by God with an unending love.

Often you hear of people who say, "I'm just not good enough to be a Christian." The response to that statement is, "Welcome to the club. None of us are." The love of God is long.

How wide is His love? Think of the rich young ruler in the Bible who came to see Jesus. When Jesus told him to sell everything he had and follow Him, the young man said he couldn't do that. Did Jesus really want him to sell all he had? No, he wanted him to understand the grace of God and that he had to love God first. Christ was saying, "I love you, but you have to come to me."

When the woman was taken in adultery, and the men were standing with stones ready to kill her, Jesus said that whoever was without sin should cast the first stone. The breadth of Christ's love included her.

Zaccheus, the tax collector who stole from people and was hated for it, was moved to repay his victims fourfold after meeting Jesus because of the love that was shown to him. God even loved Herod, Nero, Hitler, Stalin, and every other infamous person you can think of throughout history. That is how wide God's love is.

To see how deep that love is, go to Gethsemane as Jesus is praying. Go to where He took those beatings the next day and on to Golgotha where He hung on the cross for us. That is the depth of His love, but it also reaches new heights because He now is in Heaven interceding for us.

After the examination of His love, in verse 19 we see the exhibit of His love. *"And to know the love of Christ, which passeth knowledge, that ye might be filled with all the fulness of God."*

You cannot begin to comprehend how much it is that God loves us. It is beyond our knowledge, as this verse says.

There is creature love, such as a hen with her chicks. There is parental love, demonstrated by a mother with her children. There are other types of love we could discuss, but there is no greater example of love than what is mentioned in this verse, that we cannot comprehend.

As I studied these verses, I realized that there is no way the greatest orator in the world could explain this passage properly. Then I read that short phrase, *"passeth knowledge."* If you think you know how much God loves you, add something to it, and He loves you even more than that.

The evidence of His love is found in the final portion of verse 19. Isn't it wonderful to see people whose ruined lives find purpose after they come to Christ? Perhaps you came to Christ later in life. If so, you may understand His love a little bit better. Sometimes, when we are raised in church and spend nearly our entire lives there, we don't appreciate as much the love that God has for us.

Verse 20 speaks of the enablement of His love. *"Now unto him that is able to do exceeding abundantly above all that we ask or think, according to the power that worketh in us."* God not only is able to give us whatever we ask or think, but He goes beyond what we could ever ask and can even change our asking according to His power.

As we have discussed previously, the first three chapters of Ephesians show us the glorious position we have in Jesus Christ and all of the blessings we have. Now He closes this section of the book by reminding us, above everything else, that He simply loves us. It is a love that only He can give.

A final reminder of the power of God is given in verse 21. *"Unto him be glory in the church by Christ Jesus throughout all ages, world without end. Amen."* All power belongs to Him.

When I was a child going to church there was something we did every Sunday morning. It was even printed in the bulletin. First there was the Doxology, then the invocation, and the listing of the Gloria Patri.

As a kid I would often get bored listening to that stuff, but one day it dawned on me what was being said, with phrases like "Praise God from whom all blessings flow" and "Glory to God in the highest." Between these reminders about what He was and is and will be, there was a short prayer that expressed how we were meeting at the feet of a holy God.

This was what Paul was saying in these passages when he wrote, *"I bow my knees."* How wonderful it is to be able to have a relationship with God

Years ago the great evangelist D.L. Moody founded the Moody Bible Institute in Chicago, the oldest Bible college of its kind in the United States today.

Once when he was in Europe, Moody was asked by a young preacher, "Would you let me preach in your church if I ever come to America?"

Of course, any young preacher would love to fill Moody's pulpit, but Moody didn't think the man would ever show up, so he said yes.

But one day this man did show up. His name was Morehouse. A series of meetings was coming up and Moody would have to be absent for some of them, so young Morehouse was allowed to preach. As he did, there was a tremendous sense of vibrancy in that church.

When Moody came home after a few days and asked how the meetings were going, his wife replied, "Wonderful."

Moody was intrigued by his wife's enthusiastic response, so he inquired further. "What did he preach about Wednesday night?"

"John 3:16. 'For God So Loved The World.'"

"All right. What about Thursday night?"

"John 3:16."

"Friday night?"

The answer was the same.

"Well," said Moody. "Doesn't he have anything else to preach about?"

His wife looked at him and said, "Darling, I'm learning about the love of God like I've never known it before. We hear so often about the judgment of God, but not the love of God."

Moody went to church that Sunday and heard Morehouse preach, morning and evening, on John 3:16. Many came to Christ, and it so transformed Moody that he put a large neon sign out in front of the church that said, GOD IS LOVE.

One day an old drunkard was walking down the streets of Chicago and he saw those words. He thought, "That isn't true. God could never love me." He was going to keep walking, but something in the words of that sign drew him inside the church.

He took a seat in the balcony. The sanctuary was full, and another famous evangelist, R..A. Torrey, was preaching on John 3:16. The drunkard was riveted to his seat as the service ended. Torrey walked up to the balcony.

"Why aren't you leaving," Torrey asked. "The service is over."

"Because it isn't true," the man replied. "God doesn't love me. No one could ever love someone like me."

Torrey began to tell him about the height, depth, breadth and length of God's love. That drunkard not only was saved, but he helped start a rescue mission in that city to help others like him because he realized that God is love.

I remember the first time as a young preacher I counseled a married couple. They were very much in love and had just had their first big argument. All of us who are married can remember that, and there are times that we wonder, "Does he love me? Does she love me?" We know that they do, but we all struggle with that because we are human beings.

God is not like us. He loves us all of the time. As we think about our glorious identity in Christ, we must remember first and foremost that God loves us.

CHAPTER 8

DON'T SPLIT THE BABY
Ephesians 4:1-6

There is a fascinating story in the Old Testament about Solomon. Just after he became king, the Lord asked him, "What would you like to have?"

Solomon replied, "Give me wisdom and understanding."

"I am so glad you asked for that," God told him. "You did not ask for money or for power, but I will give you those things anyway in addition to wisdom and understanding."

Within a short time Solomon was put to the test. There were two harlots, or prostitutes, who were in the palace at that time and each of them had a baby. One night, while the babies slept next to their mothers, one of them died. The mother of the dead baby then switched it with the baby that was still living, and when the other mother awoke and saw the dead baby, she said, "This is not my child." So they went to the king to settle their dispute.

Each woman claimed before Solomon that the living child was hers. There was no DNA testing available at that time, but Solomon had been given wisdom and understanding from the Lord which he would use to solve this mystery.

"Go and get me a sword," the king said to his aide. As the weapon was brought to him, the people who witnessed this event likely wondered what in the world Solomon would do with a sword in this situation

"Since both of you claim this child," Solomon said to the women, "We will cut the baby in half, and then give half to each of you."

With that, the real mother spoke up. "Oh, no," she said. "Just give her the baby."

The other woman said that the king's solution was fine with her.

Solomon knew then to whom the baby belonged. He pointed to the mother and said, "Give her the baby." And she took her child and went away.

While we might not have come up with the same solution as Solomon for this situation, we would almost certainly agree with the mother who said, "Don't split the baby."

In Ephesians there is a great portion of Scripture in which God talks to us about unity in the body of Christ. When God looks at people, He sees only those who are lost and those who are saved; those who are out of the family of God, and those who are in the family of God.

Here the Lord is commanding us to never divide the body, or "split the baby." This is emphasized in verse 3 of Ephesians 4, which says, "Endeavouring to keep the unity of the Spirit in the bond of peace."

As pastor of my church, especially since it has two separate locations, I understand that one day I will stand before God and answer for the level of unity in that church. In whatever church you attend, you are also responsible before God for keeping unity in your church.

It is hard to know how well we are united and what we are united on. When you look at the church of Jesus Christ in general, around the world, it's difficult to know how to do it. For example, in some places, especially in Europe, there is the "state church." You pay your tithe to the government, which in turn gives the money to the church. There's not a lot of motivation to do much in those situations, but for many lost people that is how the church operates.

For others, there are non-conformist groups. These say, "We're all by ourselves, and nobody is to get near us." Think of all the denominations. There are Presbyterians, Methodists, Catholics, Baptists, charismatics, and many others.

Then, in the area of Bible prophecy, there are all kinds of ideas. What most of us say is, "My idea is the right one; the rest of you are wrong." There are the post-millenialists who believe that the world is ready to bring in the Kingdom. There are a-millenialists who say that we are to be spiritually fulfilled, and that is how the Kingdom will be brought in. There are pre-millenialists, like me, who believe in a literal Kingdom here on Earth. Then you have pre-tribulation, mid-tribulation, post-tribulation, partial rapturalists. After a while, you begin to wonder what is right. Then you talk to unsaved people, and their eyes start to cross and they say, "I have no idea what you are talking about."

One of the interesting things about these types of situations is that some people understand that unity is a part of the body of Christ, but the question for many is, "What exactly brings about this unity?" There are churches that argue incessantly about the color of the carpet, the color of the walls, what kind of building they should have and whether there should be a steeple. You probably realize that, in 100 years, none of these things are going to matter. So what kind of unity is God talking about in these verses?

A few years ago I visited the great Metropolitan Tabernacle when I was preaching in England. That church was pastored in the 19th century by Charles Haddon Spurgeon, and for many years thousands attended every week. The auditorium there is now fairly small, and the church is being led by a pastor named Peter Masters, who is doing a good job.

As I walked in I saw a large bust of Spurgeon, and I considered that statue while thinking about how much they talk about the past at that church. So I asked, "What about the future here?"

My home church in south Florida has been in existence for more than 50 years, and I thank God for its great history. But I constantly challenge my people to think about the future. I would say the same to you today, and at the same time I ask you to consider this: What unites us?

Look at Ephesians 4 and you will see a word that keeps coming up in these chapters. The word is *walk*. Verse 1 tells us to *"walk worthy of the vocation wherewith ye are called."* Verse 17 says, *"… that ye henceforth walk not as other Gentiles walk,"*

Eph. 5:2 commands us to *"walk in love."* In that same chapter, verse 8 says we are to *"walk as children of light."* Then, in verse 15, we are to *"see that you walk circumspectly."*

There are six Greek terms that are translated into *walk* in the New Testament. In each case, it speaks about physically walking, but it signifies the road traveled by an individual in his life. God is saying, "Here is how you should live and how you should walk." In other words, we should become more and more like Him so that people who see our walk also see Him and want to know what He is all about.

In verse 2 of the fourth chapter of Ephesians we see four characteristics of this walk: *"With all lowliness and meekness, with long-suffering, forbearing one another in love."* In this passage *lowliness* means humility of mind, and it suggests the thoughts of God's wisdom, love, and power. It means to put an end to pride.

Meekness refers to cultivating the spirit of the Lord. *Longsuffering* is being patient with one another, and *forbearing* is putting up with each other in the body of Christ, and all our idiosyncrasies and the faults that we so quickly can see in other people.

Have you noticed that you don't have to be with someone very long before you find something about which the two of you can disagree? I think about my own relationship with my wife. I think a steak should be medium well; she thinks it should be medium rare. I can't imagine eating meat that way. She'll order something in a restaurant and I wonder how in the world she could eat that particular dish, but she seems to like it.

Sometimes you can be around a person long enough that you think, "I don't want to associate with this person anymore. We are too different." But God is telling us in these passages that in the body of Christ we have something that unites us and we must never split the baby.

As we have stated several times, the first three chapters of Ephesians talk about our position in Christ, or our spiritual identification. From there, the remaining chapters tell us how to put into practice what we are. In other words, chapters 1-3 show us our worth in Christ, while chapters 4-6 teach us how to walk in Christ. First we learn the doctrine, or what we believe; then we see our duty, or how we are to respond. In every case, the absence of these qualities may jeopardize our unity in the body of Christ.

Look at John 17:21. This is Jesus' prayer to the Father before He went to the cross, and He makes a major request: *"That they all may be one; as thou, Father, art in me, and I in thee, that they also may be one in us: that the world may believe that thou hast sent me."*

He is saying here that there must be unity within the body of Christ so that people who do not know Him will understand that God sent Jesus and have a better grasp of who we are in Christ.

A few years ago I was asked to preach in a series of meetings in Romania. This was just after Romania had come away from communism, when Ceausescu had been killed, and the people were experiencing a newfound freedom they were beginning to enjoy. I went to one church whose leaders told me they were a-millenialists.

"We want you to preach and teach us what you believe about the pre-tribulationist, pre-millenial return of Christ, so our people will understand that," they said.

I was thrilled to do that, because I believe that is the right way. But if they had never changed their minds, they would still be part of the body of Christ. These people had been through some severe persecution, as have Christians in other nations in the past century, and they knew others who had died for their faith. Some scholars believe that there have been more martyrs in our present-day world than at any time in the history of Christianity. So if these Romanians did not believe everything exactly as I believe it, they would still be part of the body of Christ.

Now look back at Ephesians 4, beginning with the first verse. *"I therefore, the prisoner of the Lord, beseech you that ye walk worthy of the vocation wherewith ye are called,"* Paul writes. He is at this time in prison, where he cannot preach, but he can pray and he can write. He is telling us to walk properly according to our calling.

That brings us back to verse 2, which, as we saw earlier, ends with these words: *"In love."* Ephesians 3 talks about the height, breadth and depth of the love of God, and we are to show that same love to each other.

Verse 3 says, *"Endeavouring to keep the unity of the Spirit in the bond of peace."* The word *endeavouring* means to keep at it, and *bond* means a strengthening of peace that increases when we clasp that which will ensure our God-given ability to have peace in the body of Christ.

Here is the bottom line: You and I as Christians need to be studying and striving to be more and more like Jesus Christ. Sometimes we talk about how we want to become more like someone in the Bible or someone we know, but our goal should be to become more like Christ.

This passage shows us why those who belong to Christ should be eager to preserve their unity, and we see this in three areas.

Look at verse 4: *"There is one body, and one Spirit, even as ye are called in one hope of your calling."* Notice that there is a single, visible community, and the Bible says that it is not a mystical concept but rather true believers who are together in Jesus Christ. There are men, women, boys and girls who have trusted Jesus and are part of the body of Christ.

When other churches are rejoicing in good things that happen in their midst, we should not be jealous of them, but we should rejoice with them. I recently got an e-mail from a church in Liberia, in west Africa. They found our church's Web site and modeled much of what they are doing after us. They named their church after ours – New Testament Baptist Church. The man who wrote the e-mail asked me to send him some books, tapes and other materials. That is how the various members of the body of Christ work together.

When you are saved, there is only one *Spirit* that lives in you, and that is the Holy Spirit. Romans 8:9 says, *"If any man have not the spirit of Christ, he is not his."*

The *hope* that is referred to in Eph. 4:4 is a confident expectation. The definition of hope in the English dictionary is "a feeling for that which we want to happen." But that is not the Bible definition of that word. We don't doubt for one single moment that Jesus Christ is coming again. He said He was coming again, and we shall see Him, we shall be like Him, for we shall see Him as He is.

We believe in the local church, and there are many churches that are going out and winning souls to Christ and serving Him. We praise God for that. But there is one body, one spirit and one hope.

The next group we should notice is in verse 5. *"One Lord, one faith, one baptism."* There are not two lords or three lords, but one – our Lord and Saviour Jesus Christ.

The city of Ephesus was not a religious center like Jerusalem, or a cultural center like Athens, or a political center like Rome. It was a place of Christian and pagan worship. For example, there was the temple of Diana. Many theologians believe that there were a large number of churches in that area whose people worshipped a variety of gods. But as this verse says, we are to have only one Lord.

There are those who say that Christians are intolerant for only having one God and one way to Heaven. But I would remind you that there is only one who died, was buried and rose again. That is why there is only one Lord.

The word *faith* here speaks about what we believe. Think for a moment about Christ, who we are to strive to be like. He is the Son of God, eternal, omnipotent, omniscient, omnipresent, holy, just, and loving. He is the second Person of the Godhead, co-equal with the Father, born of a virgin, the Victor, the resurrected One, who offers grace to us, and he was predicted by the prophets. The very essence of our faith is the person and the work of Jesus Christ.

The *baptism* can refer to spiritual baptism as well as water baptism. The first thing that Jesus did in His earthly ministry was be baptized, which is a symbol of what we are in Christ.

Now look at verse 6. *"One God and Father of all, who is above all, and through all, and in you all."* Jesus introduced the concept of God as a Father. This was not well-known prior to His ministry on Earth.

The story of the prodigal son, one of the best-known in the New Testament, refers often to the father. When Jesus ascended into Heaven, He said, "Wait for the promise of the Father." This would be the Holy Spirit.

Jesus is the Shepherd, the Rock, a shield, the Holy One of Israel. But He is also the One through which we have access to the Father, who is *"above all,"* according to this verse.

He rules the galaxies. There is no government on Earth that can rule outside of His decree, and He will ultimately be seen as having all power in this world

He is also *through all*, which means He is "passing through all." When Jesus went to the cross, a lot of people thought, "Well, that's the end of him. He's dead." But He wasn't dead for long. He was just passing through.

When He was placed in the tomb, more people shrugged and went on their way, thinking it was over. But it didn't end in the tomb. He was just passing through.

The Bible says that He rose again, and people saw Him and wondered about Him. He ascended into Heaven, but not to simply forget about us. He is passing through, and one day He will return to get us and take us home.

Finally, *in you all* means that God remains there through the Person of the Holy Spirit. Thus, the Father, Son and Holy Spirit are all working in our lives. Christianity has divergent opinions on some matters, but if you love the Lord, there will be a deep, genuine effort in your life to always strive for unity in the body of Christ.

Here is some practical advice for you. Consider these seven things:

1. All of us are on a spiritual journey. Your knowledge of the Word of God, and your understanding of Christ and who He is, varies based upon the length of time you have been saved and growing in the Lord, but every one of us is on a spiritual journey. Our journey is leading us to Heaven, but it can be a wonderful time here on Earth when we understand that we are taking this journey in Christ. Stop and ask yourself, "Where am I on my spiritual journey? How far along am I?"

2. We will never agree on everything. That's the way life is. There have been great theologians and Bible scholars who differed on certain aspects of the Bible, but on the basics they are the same.

3. Unity is a command from God. It is not a suggestion. If you have two or more children, you have probably sat them down together at some time and said, "We're going to work this out. You are not getting along." You do that because unity is important in the family. When a football coach calls a play, a

player might not like it, but they all had better run the play the coach calls. This is the kind of unity God expects from us

4. Unity speaks volumes to those who are seeking God. In the book of Ephesians we learn about how to live out your faith with the gifts God has given you. But you are responsible to live in such a way that those who do not know the Lord can see the unity you have.

5. As Christians, you and I are to be peacemakers and always keep the unity of the church. If there is a lack of unity, we are always responsible to do something about it.

6. In essentials, there is unity. In non-essentials, there is liberty. In all things, there must be charity. Let's talk about essentials. What does the Christian believe?

A Christian believes that the Bible is the living, infallible Word of God, a Book that tells us exactly what God wants us to know. Whether you are reading Leviticus, or Matthew, or Revelation, you are reading God's word. Our opinions about God don't go very far in light of His word.

Another essential is our belief that Jesus Christ is the Son of God. There is no way to the Father but through the Person of Jesus Christ. That is the essence of the Christian faith. Jesus was born of a virgin, lived a perfect life without sin, died a vicarious death for you and me, was buried and rose again. That is essential to the Christian faith, and when we see this the Bible begins to open up to us and we see new things because of Him. That means so much when a loved one dies or you go through a crisis in life. It also helps you understand your purpose in life, that God has a plan for you.

We believe that Jesus Christ is coming again. It is what we call the blessed hope of the church.

7. Uniformity has everyone looking and thinking alike. If you ever go somewhere and see people whose clothes and hair are the same, or who stand and talk alike, that is uniformity. Unanimity is complete agreement across the board. In matters of church business, for example, there is often a need for unanimity among the leadership of the church.

Unity refers to one heart, a similarity of purpose, and agreement on the major points of doctrine. That it what Christianity is all about, but I believe the message of unity is seldom heard in today's churches. When we understand unity, we understand what the body of Christ is all about and we can bring people into the family of God with that understanding as well.

God gave Solomon great wisdom. Soon after He did that, the great challenge came: Two women, but just one baby. Who did the baby belong to?

Solomon knew that the real mother would not split the baby, but her maternal instincts would take over. So he called for the sword, and the mother of that child did as he expected. She would have given up her baby rather than see it killed.

If we love Jesus, we must understand that we as the body of Christ can make a difference in the world in which we live.

Recently I took about two dozen of our staff aside for an all-day prayer meeting. I said, "We are not going to pray for the church, or even for each other. Instead, we are going to talk to God about what He is saying to us." So each of us began to pray, "Lord, what are you saying to me? What are you trying to teach me?"

When you do that enough, you find yourself on fire for God, because He is speaking directly to you – not just about things, but about Him and who He is.

Families across our nation need to unite. Our churches need to unite for the cause of Christ. We need to say that, by the grace of God, we believe something important and we must unite to get the word out to a lost world. It's not just what we believe that is important, but what the Bible tells us about God that is most important – that Jesus Christ is the way, the truth and the life, and no one comes to the Father except through Him.

Individual churches will continue to teach their theology and what they believe. But the body of Christ, as great as it is in a single church, is even greater around the world. As you travel to other countries, you will meet people and come away feeling like you've known them for a long time. That is the body of Christ. There is a connection, and you realize that you connect because you are in the family of God.

CHAPTER 9

HOW THE BABY GROWS
Ephesians 4:7-16

_ᏧᎴ_

B abies are a delight, aren't they?
Recently I held one of my grandchildren in my arms, and she
was four months of age at the time, but it seemed as though she was
talking only to me.

As that child continues to grow, if she develops normally, I fully
expect her to speak audibly to me in a few years using words we
both understand. Then she will move to adolescence and on to the
teenage years, maneuvering during that critical time between childhood and adulthood. Finally, with all of our children, we see them
become adults, after starting so many years earlier as babies.

There is an important point to be made here. Up to now, in the
book of Ephesians, Paul has been writing about what is best for the
body of Christ. Now he is shifting gears a bit and focusing on what
is best for you and me as individuals.

Stop and think for a moment about the day that you came to
Christ, and then think about where you are right now. As a Christian,
are you an infant, a child, an adolescent, a teenager, or an adult?
That is what the Apostle Paul wants us to consider as we study this
portion of the Word of God.

A portion of Ephesians points out to us that as we grow physically, we should also grow spiritually, and there are three words in

this passage that outline how we should grow spiritually. These are easy words to remember.

The first word is **grace**. As Eph. 4:7 says, *"But unto every one of us is given grace according to the measure of the gift of Christ."* We do not grow simply because of a set of standards or rules that we keep, but we grow because of the grace of God.

Grace is the undeserved favor of God, and He has given us all that we need. About 150 times in the New Testament we find the Greek word *karos*, which means the grace of God. It is chilling to consider where some of us might be today without His grace.

The second word is **gifts**. The end of verse 7 refers to *"the gift of Christ,"* and in verse 8 we see that Jesus *"gave gifts unto men."* Verse 11 covers that in more detail: *"And he gave some, apostles; and some, prophets; and some, evangelists; and some, pastors and teachers."* God has given specific gifts to you and to me, and we grow in the gifts that He has given to us.

Look at verses 8-10. *"Wherefore he saith, When he ascended up on high, he led captivity captive, and gave gifts unto men. (Now that he ascended, what is it but that he also descended first into the lower parts of the earth? He that descended is the same also that ascended up far above all heavens, that he might fill all things.)"*

If you have never read those verses before, you are probably thinking, "That is a beautiful passage, but I have no idea what it is talking about." This passage in Ephesians is actually a quotation referring to something from the Old Testament. We see this in Psalm 68:18. "Thou hast ascended on high, thou hast led captivity captive: thou hast received gifts for men; yea, for the rebellious also, that the LORD God might dwell among them."

This verse is a call to God to rescue His people and vindicate them. This story, written by David, spoke about the glory of God and His goodness to Israel as He was leading them to the Promised Land. It is a picture of a soldier, a general, speaking to his people and saying, "Follow me. Go with me as we do what needs to be done."

Go back to Ps. 68:7-8 and 11-14. *"O God, when thou wentest forth before thy people, when thou didst march through the wilderness; Selah: The earth shook, the heavens also dropped at the pres-*

ence of God: even Sinai itself was moved at the presence of God, the God of Israel. ... The Lord gave the word: great was the company of those that published it. Kings of armies did flee apace: and she that tarried at home divided the spoil. Though ye have lien among the pots, yet shall ye be as the wings of a dove covered with silver, and her feathers with yellow gold. When the Almighty scattered kings in it, it was white as snow in Salmon."

These soldiers triumphed, but God went before them. There were many wars in the Old Testament, and as these generals came, and the soldiers came, many fell by the wayside. They would take up the tribute, the money, the wealth, and some of the kings would go back to their own people and distribute it among them, especially among those who fought the battle. These are the gifts that were given.

This is the background for what Paul is writing about in Ephesians 4. In verse 7 we see *"the measure of the gift of Christ,"* so the soldier, or the warrior, referred to in this passage is none other than the Lord Jesus Christ.

Verses 8-9 show how He ascended into Heaven and *"gave gifts unto men"* after he *"descended first into the lower parts of the earth."* The Son of God came to Earth, born as a baby, to those who needed Him and after He ministered on Earth they crucified Him.

I Peter 3: 18-19 says, "For Christ also hath once suffered for sins, the just for the unjust, that he might bring us to God, being put to death in the flesh, but quickened by the Spirit: By which also he went and preached unto the spirits in prison."

In the story of the rich man and Lazarus, the Bible says that Lazarus, when he died, was taken by the angels into *"Abraham's bosom."* On the cross, Christ spoke to the thief of being in *"paradise."* When Jesus died and rose again, He took those believers who had died before Him straight into Heaven, and all who since have died in Christ also go immediately into the presence of the Lord. This is how He "led captivity captive."

So Jesus descended to His birth, then descended to His death, ascended from the grave and again into Heaven. God has given great gifts to His church, but a great price was paid so that each of us can have the gifts we need to accomplish what God would have for us.

When you accepted Jesus Christ as your Saviour, God never intended for you to not have anything else to do for Him the rest of your life. God saved you for a reason. Too many times we look at the church and its pastors and leaders and say, "They are the ones who are supposed to do the work of the church," when in fact God has called all of us to another level.

Look at verses 11-12. *"And he gave some, apostles; and some, prophets; and some, evangelists; and some, pastors and teachers; For the perfecting of the saints, for the work of the ministry, for the edifying of the body of Christ."*

God has given every one of us spiritual gifts. You need to know your spiritual gifts and how they mesh with your personality type, and find out what God has for you in your life.

Romans 12 and I Corinthians 12 talk about these gifts, and in Ephesians 4 God is telling the church that He has given certain gifted people for the church. In verse 11 He lists five categories of gifted people: apostles, prophets, evangelists, pastors and teachers.

The apostles were the guides who taught the church the way it should go. The prophets guarded the church and what it was to know. Back in this time, the people did not have a complete Bible like you and I have today, so the prophets were there to tell the people, "This is what the Word of God says." They guarded the Scriptures.

The apostles went from place to place doing the work of God. The mission of the apostle is still true today, and that work is done by missionaries. However, the office of the apostle was for that day, to tell people that Jesus had risen and to guide the church in its teaching. Through this the people were learning what God wanted them to know.

The evangelists were gifted to deal with sinners in need of a Saviour. The pastor tended to the flock and the teacher taught the flock; those two worked hand in hand.

Look at Eph. 2:20. *"And are built upon the foundation of the apostles and prophets, Jesus Christ himself being the chief corner stone."* This is talking about the church. God used the apostles and prophets to guide and to guard the church at that time, but the evangelists, pastors and teachers He is still using today.

When an evangelist speaks, often there are crowds of people who come to Christ because that is the gift God has given him. Other preachers may not see scores of souls saved, but that does not diminish what they are doing because they have a different gift.

Why does a church have a pastor? The mission of a pastor is to lead a church. I was called to pastor my church in 1995, and I have tried to assemble a team of pastors to work with me because I believe that is necessary to properly lead a large church like ours. All of our pastors at our church are different. They all have different personalities.

Some people think that they go to church to get warm and fuzzy feelings from the pastors, enjoy their time in worship and teaching, and go home to wait for next Sunday. If that is your approach, you've missed the whole point.

Look at verse 12 again. The pastors are not here to do the work of God by themselves, but to equip you so that you can do it as well. Everyone in the family of God is to be equipped to do something for the Lord. The job of the gifted people in these verses is to equip you. God has given these people as His gift to the church. Their purpose is to teach others the work of the ministry, the goal being to build up the body of Christ.

Where does this lead? Look at verse 13: *"Till we all come in the unity of the faith, and of the knowledge of the Son of God, unto a perfect man, unto the measure of the stature of the fullness of Christ."* Notice how it all comes back to unity.

This knowledge is not just knowing about Christ. Eph. 5:1 says, *"Be ye therefore followers of God, as dear children."* The word *"followers"* in that verse is talking about being an imitator. So we are not just to know about Christ, but we must strive to become more Christ-like. The goal of every Christian is to be more and more like Jesus Christ.

The third word is **grow**. As Paul introduces this, he points out the dangers of growth in verse 14: *"That we henceforth be no more children, tossed to and fro, and carried about with every wind of doctrine, by the sleight of men, and cunning craftiness, whereby they lie in wait to deceive."*

He is giving three illustrations here. First is that of a child in the nursery; we are not to remain in that state, but instead we are to grow.

The next example he uses is that of the sea. My wife and I once were given a trip by a church family and we went on a cruise. We were supposed to go to Cancun, but we ended up in Cozumel. The ship's staff told us that the wind blew us to Cozumel.

The Bible says that when you accept Christ as your Saviour, it is very important that you get under the teaching of God's Word so that every wind of doctrine (and it's everywhere today) doesn't make you fall over and into it.

The final illustration in that verse actually refers to gambling. The *"sleight of men, and cunning craftiness"* describes sleight of hand or trickery with dice, and it is another warning of the dangers that lurk when you are trying to grow in the Lord.

The next two verses show how we are to display that growth. Verse 15 says, *"But speaking the truth in love, may grow up into him in all things, which is the head, even Christ."*

Truth with no love is ungracious and offensive. Speaking in love while suppressing truth is unfaithful. We must have both.

Look at verse 16: *"From whom the whole body fitly joined together and compacted by that which every joint supplieth, according to the effectual working in the measure of every part, maketh increase of the body unto the edifying of itself in love."*

These two verses speak of love and of life.

In Revelation 2 we see a passage that was written to the church at Ephesus. Verses 2-4 talk about their love for the Lord and what it should be:

"I know thy works, and thy labour, and thy patience, and how thou canst not bear them which are evil: and thou hast tried them which say they are apostles, and are not, and hast found them liars: And hast borne, and hast patience, and for my name's sake hast laboured, and hast not fainted. Nevertheless I have somewhat against thee, because thou hast left thy first love."

Verse 2 indicates that they have remained strong doctrinally, and verse 3 shows how they have stayed faithful, but it all seems hollow when we read those last few words in verse 4.

So the question we should ask ourselves at this point is, "How much do I love Jesus? Do I love Him as much now as I did when I first trusted Him? Do I love Him as much today as I did six months ago?"

Our problem is that the events of our life and the busyness of it all simply get in the way of our love for Jesus, and our passion for Him begins to wane.

On a recent Saturday I went about my usual routine for that day of the week – the bank, the dry cleaners, the grocery store – and ended up at a coffee shop to meet one of my sons. As I was waiting outside a beautiful young lady came by passing around small cups with a drink. I took one and thanked her for it, and it tasted quite good. She was advertising a new store around the corner, so I thought I'd go there.

I went inside, and there was loud music playing and a lot of activity for the grand opening. As I walked up to place my order, a lady came over and identified herself as one of the owners of the establishment, then proceeded to talk to me all about the store and this drink.

One of things she said was, "If you take this drink, you'll lose weight." I said, "I want the biggest one you've got." I didn't lose any weight, but she was so passionate and excited about this drink.

Shouldn't we be that passionate and excited about Christ today? The Bible tells us in this tremendous passage in Ephesians how Jesus descended into Hell and ascended into Heaven for us, then gave us wonderfully gifted people to equip us for the work of the Lord. How much do we love Jesus today?

Someone once said, "If obedience walks, then God talks." The more we obey the Lord, the more He shows Himself in our lives. We need to be imitators of Christ.

CHAPTER 10

UNDER NEW MANAGEMENT
Ephesians 4:17-24

———⁂———

W e're going to begin this chapter by looking back at Eph. 3:14-21.

"For this cause I bow my knees unto the Father of our Lord Jesus Christ, Of whom the whole family in heaven and earth is named, That he would grant you, according to the riches of his glory, to be strengthened with might by his Spirit in the inner man; That Christ may dwell in your hearts by faith; that ye, being rooted and grounded in love, May be able to comprehend with all saints what is the breadth, and length, and depth, and height; And to know the love of Christ, which passeth knowledge, that ye might be filled with all the fulness of God. Now unto him that is able to do exceeding abundantly above all that we ask or think, according to the power that worketh in us, Unto him be glory in the church by Christ Jesus throughout all ages, world without end. Amen."

Now we will see how those verses connect with Eph. 4:17-24.

"This I say therefore, and testify in the Lord, that ye henceforth walk not as other Gentiles walk, in the vanity of their mind. Having the understanding darkened, being alienated from the life of God through the ignorance that is in them, because of the blindness of their heart: Who being past feeling have given themselves over unto lasciviousness, to work all uncleanness with greediness. But ye have not so learned Christ; If so be that ye have heard him, and have been

taught by him, as the truth is in Jesus: That ye put off concerning the former conversation the old man, which is corrupt according to the deceitful lusts; And be renewed in the spirit of your mind; And that ye put on the new man, which after God is created in righteousness and true holiness."

When we come to Christ, we are under new management. It's not to be like it used to be. If what we read in chapter 3 is true about this great love that He has given to us, then we are under new management.

Sometimes we go to an office or a business that advertises this fact. There might be balloons and "Under New Management" signs, and a lot of activity like at a grand opening, with the business owner trying to convey the idea that he or she has something really good to offer you. It's like the honeymoon stage of a business. Sometimes when an existing business gains a new boss it has the same effect. New management means that we, as employees and customers, expect something to be different.

The verses we just read in Ephesians 4 are very confrontational. They hit you right between the eyes. The Bible is saying here that if God has done all of these wonderful things for us, then this is how we ought to live. Things are supposed to be different.

There are some key words in this passage that will help us better understand what we are looking at. The first one is *"walk"* in verse 17. Verse 1 of this chapter says that we are to *"walk worthy of the vocation wherewith ye are called."* Ephesians 5 uses this word several times, encouraging us to *"walk in love"* (verse 2), *"walk as children of light"* (verse 8) and *"walk circumspectly"* (verse 15). It is fairly obvious that God expects a certain type of walk in the Christian life.

The word used here signifies the whole round of activities in the lifestyle of a Christian. In other words, a Christian is supposed to be living a certain way.

We all are familiar with the adage, "If it looks like a duck, and walks like a duck, and quacks like a duck, it must be a duck." It's not a fox, or a dog, or a cat. So when the Bible says we should walk a certain way, we need to consider how our walk shows that there is something different in our lives.

The second word is *"fill,"* as in *"filled with the Spirit,"* which we see in Eph. 5:18. Of course, this refers to something being filled up. Whenever the Bible talks about being filled with the Spirit, it always carries with it a prerequisite of being filled with the Word of God. They go hand in hand.

The filling of the Word of God is pointed out in Col. 3:16-17. *"Let the word of Christ dwell in you richly in all wisdom; teaching and admonishing one another in psalms and hymns and spiritual songs, singing with grace in your hearts to the Lord. And whatsoever ye do in word or deed, do all in the name of the Lord Jesus, giving thanks to God and the Father by him."*

The third word is *"testify,"* seen in Eph. 4:17. The word used here means to be summoned like a witness. When you are asked to give your testimony, you do so by testifying. You are witnessing to someone about what God has done in your life.

The Christian worldview clashes with all other worldviews. It is inevitable. The testimony of a Christian is radically different from that of someone who does not know Jesus Christ. You and I as Christians will never be satisfied on the inside until we have had a testimony.

We read all through Ephesians about the grace of God and how wonderful it is. If you think of grace only as a ticket to Heaven, then you are missing out on what the Apostle Paul is trying to teach us here. In Eph. 4:20 he says as much: "But ye have not so learned Christ."

When you focus on your performance and what a good job you think you are doing as a Christian, you will find that God is interested in that. When we focus on performing the Christian life, it becomes lifeless and empty after a while. But when we become obsessed with our service, it literally energizes us and reinforces the fact that there is a divine life living within us.

For example, a husband and wife come into my office and announce that they are having marital troubles. The husband says to her, "I don't feel like you love me anymore."

She becomes outraged. "I clean the dishes, mop the floor, take care of your clothes, tend to the baby – what are you talking about? I don't think you love me."

Then it's his turn. "I work 10-12 hours a day to provide for our family. How can you suggest that I don't love you?"

All that these two are talking about is what "I" do.

You can serve Christ by teaching, or feeding the hungry, or singing in the choir, or any of a hundred other things and still be focusing only on what you are doing. You are "performing" and not really in love with Jesus.

We need to become obsessed with the divine life of Christ. We can see in Phil. 2:5-8 the example Christ set for us. *"Let this mind be in you, which was also in Christ Jesus: Who, being in the form of God, thought it not robbery to be equal with God: But made himself of no reputation, and took upon him the form of a servant, and was made in the likeness of men: And being found in fashion as a man, he humbled himself, and became obedient unto death, even the death of the cross."*

Theologians call this teaching the "kenosis," which comes from the word *kinou*, meaning to empty oneself. Here is what it means.

During Jesus' earthly ministry, He never ceased to be God, but He was also a man. Many times He could have done things as God but He chose to do them as a man. When He went to the cross, He could have called legions of angels to protect Him but did not. It was the emptying of His deity, although He never stopped being God.

Jesus often said while on Earth that He was here to do what His Father wanted. The book of John gives several examples of Christ's submission to the will of the Father:

"I can of mine own self do nothing" (John 5:30).

"My doctrine is not mine, but his that sent me" (John 7:16).

"I do nothing of myself; but as my Father hath taught me, I speak these things" (John 8:28).

"Neither came I of myself, but he sent me" (John 8:42).

Jesus could, as God, do whatever He wanted to do, but He laid that aside. In doing so, He was the perfect example of how we follow God's will and His leadership.

Look at John 15:4-5. "Abide in me, and I in you. As the branch cannot bear fruit of itself, except it abide in the vine; no more can ye, except ye abide in me. I am the vine, ye are the branches: He that abideth in me, and I in him, the same bringeth forth much fruit: for without me ye can do nothing."

It's not about us working and performing for God, because without Him we can do nothing. It's about a relationship with Him. Christianity is not a call to living through some principles that are laid out for us to follow, but it is Christ working through our lives.

A great book written in the 1800s by Charles Sheldon titled *In His Steps* asked the simple question, "What would Jesus do?" The idea of the book was to ask that question in every circumstance of life. That is exactly what Christianity is really all about.

To understand what it means to live under new management, we need to consider how old business is conducted. The last phrase of Eph. 4:17 refers to those who walk *"in the vanity of their mind."* This phrase suggests an apostasy, almost an anti-God mentality. If we are in Christ but continue living in our old ways, we live a life of absolute futility.

Verse 18 speaks about the mind being *"darkened, being alienated from the life of God."* II Cor. 4:4 speaks about the idea that we can be blinded by the devil himself, and religion does not make up the answer.

Doing business the old way demonstrates *"the ignorance that is in them, because of the blindness of their heart."* God does not want to be alienated, but to inhabit our lives.

A recent article in Newsweek highlighted a conversation with Rick Warren and an atheist. Warren asked him, "Do you believe in the Spirit?" The man talked about the possibility from a metaphysical standpoint, and then Warren went on to discuss immortality and other matters. This exchange made it clearer than ever to me that we are all empty until Christ rules in our lives. Even if you claim not to believe in God, you will always sense that emptiness.

Verse 19 takes this a step further, with some very interesting words. *"Who being past feeling have given themselves over unto lasciviousness, to work all uncleanness with greediness."* People who get further and further from Christ can get to the point where, as God tries to speak to them, they aren't even sure what they believe anymore.

I have an excellent dentist who has put a lot of Novocain into my mouth over the years. He has a way of doing it so that I don't even feel the needle going in, and soon I get very numb so he can work on me. When the feeling comes back, everything is fine because the Novocain was in during the procedure and I am *"past feeling."* We can reach a similar level of numbness spiritually if we are not careful.

The *"work"* in the last portion of the verse refers to an occupation, and we all know what *"greediness"* means. For too many of us, our god in this day and age is money.

You might come to church one Sunday, meet someone who gives you a check for $10,000 and leave the service feeling better than when you arrived. Or, you could come and hear about how we abide in Christ and He in us, and you feel no different after that than before.

Christianity is not a creed, although many creeds have been written about it and some of those are very good. Christianity is not a code of living, although such a code might have some good to it. Christianity is not a philosophy, or theology, or even a discipline.

Christianity is Christ living His life through you. It is not just doing good or "performing."

It is summed up in verse 20: *"But ye have not so learned Christ."* Being under new management means life in Christ.

Verse 21 says, *"If so be that ye have heard him, and have been taught by him, as the truth is in Jesus."* There are three key words in that verse. The word *"heard"* means to listen and obey; the word *"taught"* means learning not with man's wisdom but with God's wisdom; and the word *"truth"* means to deal faithfully.

Remember when Christ asked Pilate, "What is truth?" This passage says that Jesus Himself is truth.

Verse 22 goes back to old management again: *"That ye put off concerning the former conversation the old man, which is corrupt according to the deceitful lusts."* Are you living as you were before salvation? Is there a difference or a transformation in you since you were saved? Do you look at life differently, or are you still under old management?

Bible commentator John Phillips gave a great illustration regarding this. He saw a sign at a dry cleaning business that read, "If your clothes are not becoming to you, they should be coming to us." We should be taking off the old clothes and putting on the new.

Verses 23-24 talk about how we should be putting on something that is brand-new. *"And be renewed in the spirit of your mind; And that ye put on the new man, which after God is created in righteousness and true holiness."* There is no one in the world who can satisfy your soul like Jesus, and no one is comparable to Him.

I went out recently and participated in a fishing tournament in support of our Christian school. The group of men I was with had a great time and I caught a few fish, including a seven-pound dolphin.

When we came in to weigh our fish, I got my picture taken with that dolphin just like everyone else. As I was walking away, I saw two huge men carrying the biggest dolphin I had ever seen in my life. It weighed 46 pounds. Anything that comes out of the water at 46 pounds is big. Suddenly I wanted to hide my dolphin. "It doesn't compare to theirs," I thought.

There is no one, anywhere, at any time, who can compare to our Lord. He is the only One like Him. So when we talk about putting on Christ, we aren't putting on legalistic laws or a creed or a code, but the life of Christ is being lived in our lives. People will recognize us for who we are, because Christians who are Christ-like display Christ in their lives.

When you go through heartache or distress, you know that Jesus is there to comfort you and give you strength. When you need hope, you realize that He can give you hope. When your best friend has left you, you know that Jesus is there.

But when people out in the world know that you are in Christ, they expect you to be different because Jesus is living within you.

Go back to Psalm 17:15. The psalmist, David, is writing about his confidence in the final salvation of God. *"As for me, I will behold thy face in righteousness: I shall be satisfied, when I awake, with thy likeness."* One day we will be able to see our Lord face to face. The essence of the Christian life is affirming that Jesus is the One we seek to know and love above everyone else.

This should be our prayer: "I affirm that you, Jesus, are my life. From this day forward, I will seek to know you above all else."

Think about those words. There are a lot of other things in our lives. We have spouses and children, work, money, business, travel – so many things we are involved with. Can you truly offer those words in sincerity to the Lord?

As a young man, I was preaching at a conference in Albany, New York. We gathered for a supper in the basement of the church before going upstairs for the service where I would speak. An elderly man went up the stairs with me after the meal, and as he was laboring to take one step at a time I slowed down to talk with him.

We exchanged the customary pleasantries and I asked him if his wife was with him that night. "No," he said. "She is in Heaven."

"I'm sorry," I replied.

"Don't be sorry. She's in Heaven."

I asked him if he had any children living nearby. "No. I had children, but they are all in Heaven," he said.

Again I said, "I'm sorry."

"I told you not to say you were sorry. They're all fine. They're in Heaven."

Finally I asked him if he had any relatives, and he told me they were all in Heaven. This time I did not say I was sorry. But I will never forget the next thing he said to me.

"I have found my life to be full in Christ," he said. "This church family has become my family. Don't worry about me. I'm doing fine."

You must have a real commitment to Christ and be in love with Him to say something like that.

CHAPTER 11

HURTING GOD
Ephesians 4:25-32

Is it possible to actually hurt God in your life?

Let's look at Eph. 4:25-32. *"Wherefore putting away lying, speak every man truth with his neighbour: for we are members one of another. Be ye angry, and sin not: let not the sun go down upon your wrath: Neither give place to the devil. Let him that stole steal no more: but rather let him labour, working with his hands the thing which is good, that he may have to give to him that needeth. Let no corrupt communication proceed out of your mouth, but that which is good to the use of edifying, that it may minister grace unto the hearers. And grieve not the holy Spirit of God, whereby ye are sealed unto the day of redemption. Let all bitterness, and wrath, and anger, and clamour, and evil speaking, be put away from you, with all malice: And be ye kind one to another, tenderhearted, forgiving one another, even as God for Christ's sake hath forgiven you."* How wonderful that God has forgiven us.

God has placed all of us on Earth for a reason. God has a purpose for your life, and that is why you are here. You are on a mission from God.

The prophet Jeremiah put it so well in Jer. 29:11, which says, *"For I know the thoughts that I think toward you, saith the LORD, thoughts of peace, and not of evil, to give you an expected end."* God has a future and a hope for you and your life.

Eccl. 3:11 says, *"He hath made every thing beautiful in his time: also he hath set the world in their heart, so that no man can find out the work that God maketh from the beginning to the end."* God has made us not only for an earthly life, but also for eternity. We should not hinder His purpose or stand in the way of what He has for us in our lives, but sometimes we do.

If you have two or more children, you understand how they can argue and fuss with each other. If that goes on long enough, it hurts you as a parent. "I wish they could get along better," you say.

God is the same way. We can hurt God. The word we are using here for "hurt" means to grieve, to cause pain, or to stress. As Eph. 4:30 points out, we are given specific instructions not to grieve the Holy Spirit.

When you accepted Jesus Christ as your Saviour, although you may not have realized it at the time, the Holy Spirit came to live within you. But you can hurt the work and the ministry of the Holy Spirit. You can literally hurt God.

When we think of God, we think of Him being sovereign and righteous, mighty and powerful, and He is certainly all of those things. But as these verses teach us, we can hurt Him. I Thess. 5:19 talks about quenching the Holy Spirit, which means to put out His power.

When you see someone with passion for the Lord, don't tell that person to calm down or get rid of that passion. Thank God for it, and if you have a passion for God today you should thank Him for that.

In verses 25 and 31 there are two words that tell us something God wants us to do. Both of these verses contain the words *"put away."* In these instances it is the same term that is used when talking about divorce. In other words, there are some things in our lives that God wants us to completely separate from.

Verses 25-29 show us certain actions we need to put away. Verse 31 refers to certain attitudes that should be put away. But that is immediately followed in verse 32 by three attributes that we need to put on.

When you accepted Christ, it was a wonderful event. If you have only been saved a short time you remember vividly what it was like. When a new convert sees someone who has been a Christian for a long time but is not living the right way, the new Christian begins to wonder why. God wants those of us who come to Him to be transformed people. We shouldn't be like we used to be; something has happened, and we should be different.

You will recall that the first three chapters of Ephesians taught us how many great things God has done for us. Now we see how, because of that, we must be careful not to grieve or hurt the Holy Spirit.

Let's look at the five actions listed here that we are instructed to put away. The first one, mentioned in verse 25, is lying.

It is so easy for any of us, in an unguarded moment when confronted with an awkward question, to take refuge in a lie. You might even be uncomfortable simply reading these words right now because we have all told a lie at one time or another.

My mother was old-fashioned in many ways when it came to rearing children, and she believed in strict discipline. She told me once, "If you lie, I'm going to wash your mouth out with soap." She thought lying was important enough to merit that kind of warning.

Lying comes straight from the devil. The Bible says in John 8:44 that the devil is the father of all lies.

When the children of Israel left Egypt and eventually reached the Promised Land, God reminded them that they were to speak the truth. They had to be honest and truthful to remain in Canaan. Zechariah 8:16 says, "These are the things that ye shall do; Speak ye every man the truth to his neighbour; execute the judgment of truth and peace in your gates."

If your life is a lie, or if you are always telling lies, at some point you begin to lose the blessing and anointing of God, because you are grieving and hurting the work of the Holy Spirit.

The second thing to put away is found in verse 26. *"Be ye angry, and sin not: let not the sun go down upon your wrath."* The first three words look good to many of us. We would love an excuse to be angry.

God is not saying here that it is bad to have anger; in fact, there are times in the Bible where we find that God Himself was angry. For example, Jesus went into the temple shortly before He was crucified and found men there gambling away their money. They were selling animals to be used as sacrifices, but in doing so they were cheating people. So Jesus cleaned the place out.

Eph. 5:1 says, *"Be ye therefore followers of God, as dear children."* It is OK to get angry once in a while, but don't sin while you do it. You are possibly wondering right now, "What in the world is he talking about?"

My wife received some land in northern Pennsylvania from her father. It's a nice piece of land, and she has always taken care of it since it was in her family. Occasionally there are things that need to be done, such as wood removed from the property, and since we live so far away now she will do business by phone from time to time.

One day I came home while she was on the phone and I could tell that the call was very tense. I walked up to her and mouthed the words, "What's going on?" She didn't want me to know, so she waved me off and made it clear that she didn't want me to listen.

I went into the other room and picked up another extension so I could listen. The man on the other end of the line, who was working out a deal to remove some wood from the property, was getting very angry with my wife. He came very close to threatening her.

If there is one thing most Italians have, it's a quick temper. I exploded on the phone. "I don't know who you are, but I'm coming after you," I said. "Where do you live?" The man lived five hours away.

Of course, I had no idea what this guy looked like. He could have been a giant lumberjack. But no one is going to talk to my wife like that.

"Don't ever call this house and talk like that again," I warned him. My wife kept trying to get me to stop, but I wasn't going to put up with that kind of behavior.

Was I wrong in reacting like that? I don't think so. There are times when we have to be angry. The other day I saw on television some footage of Buddhist monks fighting with each other. I don't know what it was all about, but everyone gets angry from time to time.

Some of you reading this have probably had a big fight with your spouse on a Saturday, gone to bed, gotten up the next morning and gone to church with a happy face, ready to get back home after the service and start up the fight again. That's the kind of anger this verse is talking about. It's a good thing to make certain you go to bed at night with a quiet spirit.

A great verse that communicates this thought is Ps. 4:4. *"Stand in awe, and sin not: commune with your own heart upon your bed, and be still."* When you go to bed at night, stop for a moment and think about whether you are right with your spouse, your children, and everyone else in your life, and things are as they should be.

Today we have anger management counseling, which is a good thing because some people in our society can easily get very angry. It's one thing to get angry, but whatever you do, don't live your life sinning with that anger.

Right after these thoughts in Ephesians 4 is verse 27: *"Neither give place to the devil."* This is talking about your testimony.

Sin did not begin in the Garden of Eden with Adam and Eve. Sin really began in Heaven with Lucifer, the highest-anointed angel. Satan is not our friend.

Eph. 2:21-22 says, *"In whom all the building fitly framed together groweth unto an holy temple in the Lord: In whom ye also are builded together for an habitation of God through the Spirit."* That temple in verse 21 is you.

Now look back in Ephesians 4, at verses 2 and 16. *"With all lowliness and meekness, with longsuffering, forbearing one another in love ... From whom the whole body fitly joined together and compacted by that which every joint supplieth, according to the effectual working in the measure of every part, maketh increase of the body unto the edifying of itself in love."*

We are always in spiritual warfare. Every day of our lives we are faced with issues that, if you are not careful, will preoccupy your mind and take you away from the best that God has for you. That's why God reminds us here not to give place to the devil.

The point that is made in verse 28 is a fairly simple one. *"Let him that stole steal no more: but rather let him labour, working with his hands the thing which is good, that he may have to give to him that needeth."*

When you come to Christ, there needs to be repentance in your life. That means you turn from sin and toward Christ; there is a change of mind that leads to a change of actions. Some people say that they've come to Christ but they keep living the same way they did before.

If you stole things as a lost person, you know now that stealing is wrong because the Holy Spirit tells you. So you stop doing what you did before. That's what this verse is talking about.

Look at the next part of the verse. Why do we work for a living? We do it so we can give our tithes and offerings to the Lord and so we can take care of our families. These are good things. But the final phrase of this verse gives a specific reason for our work: to be able to give to those who have needs.

I Tim. 6:17-18 says, *"Charge them that are rich in this world, that they be not highminded, nor trust in uncertain riches, but in the living God, who giveth us richly all things to enjoy; That they do good, that they be rich in good works, ready to distribute, willing to communicate."*

Do you know why God blesses? He does that so we may share some of our abundance with those who don't have what we have.

The fifth thing the Lord tells us to put off is in verse 29 of Ephesians 4. *"Let no corrupt communication proceed out of your mouth, but that which is good to the use of edifying, that it may minister grace unto the hearers."*

The word *"corrupt"* in that verse means "putrid." It describes a decaying animal or vegetable, and is used to illustrate the fact that nothing destroys a testimony more quickly than the things we may say.

Verse 31 shows us five attitudes God wants us to put away. *"Let all bitterness, and wrath, and anger, and clamour, and evil speaking, be put away from you, with all malice."*

I want to encourage you to be very careful with bitterness. It is the opposite of sweetness, coming from the Greek word *pikros*, which means pricking as with a pin. If you stick a pin into the skin of your arm, you will automatically jerk your arm back because it pricks. You could also compare it to a paper cut you might get from opening an envelope. It is referring here to a pricking of the spirit.

Sometimes we really struggle with God because we do not understand why God has allowed certain things in our lives. For instance, we pray over and over for someone to be healed, while another person prays for a friend to be healed. The other person's friend is healed and our friend is not, and we say, "God, why did you allow that to happen?" If we are not careful, this kind of thinking can let bitterness creep into our lives.

One thing I believe we must do as children of God is to declare, once and for all, that God makes no mistakes. God is sovereign, and He is in charge of all things. If we know that is true, then there is no reason to build up bitterness in our lives.

Later in the verse we see a reference to *"evil speaking."* That means "slanderous or injurious talk." The word "blasphemy" comes from this, and in I Tim. 6:4 it is called *"railing."* Mark 15:29 calls it *"mocking of Christ."* It is referring to the way we tend to talk about people.

Be careful how you talk about other Christians or what you might think about them. If it is truly a serious matter, sit down with that person one on one. Don't talk behind someone's back.

Have you ever overheard someone talking and had no idea they were talking about you in such a bad way? You thought to yourself, "I never knew they thought that way about me." That's what God is talking about here.

The last two words of verse 31, *"with malice,"* refer to a vicious disposition, or the idea of getting back at someone. The best illustration I can think of for this is an incident several years ago when I went to sleep in a motel after speaking in a meeting in another city. The faucet made an incessant "drip, drip, drip" noise, and after I got up to tighten the faucet, it would start dripping again after I lay back down. This happened several times, and when I finally got it turned off, I lay awake half the night wondering when it would start up again. That's what malice is like – it's the idea of not letting go.

Have you had something happen with your spouse or in your family and you refuse to let them forget about it? That is malice. Like the other attitudes listed here, it can not only hurt you, but can also hurt God.

Now look at verse 32, which shows us three attributes we should take on. *"And be ye kind one to another, tenderhearted, forgiving one another, even as God for Christ's sake hath forgiven you."*

The Greek word in that verse for *"kind"* literally means "sweet and generous," having the right kind of disposition. But this can be tough.

The Bible says that we are to weep when others weep and rejoice with those who rejoice. I find that it's not hard to weep with those who weep, who come and ask me to pray with them over a loved one or a problem. Your heart goes out to that. It's a lot harder to hear from someone who is having something great happen financially, for instance, and you grit your teeth while saying to them, "That's wonderful." You wonder why such good fortune doesn't happen to you, and that leads to complaining. But God wants us to be kind across the board, whether the person in question is in a valley or on a mountaintop. That is Christ-like.

The word *"tenderhearted"* here means "full of pity." Hippocrates once talked about the healthy function of the intestines, which in this day was often referred to as the seat of the emotions, and this phrase talks about having such a deep level of compassion.

But the most important point in this verse is that we should forgive one another, because God has forgiven us. We do not deserve to be forgiven by God, but I am so glad He forgives us anyway. Forgiveness is available to anyone and everyone, but to receive it you must become closely identified with the Person of Jesus Christ.

The opening verses of Ephesians 5, which we will cover in the next chapter, instruct us to be imitators of Christ and to *"walk in love,"* or become more and more like our Lord Jesus. It was said of the early Christian church by many historians that the one thing which really identified them was their ability to love each other.

If you get at odds with someone in your church or another church, or within your family if all are Christians, you must understand that you are hurting yourself, hurting others and hurting God. That is what grieving the Holy Spirit is all about. Instead, we need a free-flowing sense of Christ and His Spirit working through us.

If you go to the Sea of Galilee, you will agree that it is one of the most beautiful areas in the Holy Land. There is life there, beautiful fish in the sea, and foliage all around at certain times of the year. It is a gorgeous spot. I have been on trips where a group of people would take a boat ride out to the middle of the sea and stop for a worship service, which is a beautiful thing.

Then you go south to Masada and eventually the Dead Sea. That body is full of salt and is like a desert. You will not see rich foliage or fish in the water. That is because there is no egress where the Jordan River runs into the Dead Sea, or no place for it to flow back out.

You can put whatever you want of God and His word into your life, but if you are not giving it back out, your faith becomes dead. Is your life rich and alive with passion for Christ? Aren't you glad that Christ died, rose again and is coming back for you one day? If we trust and follow Him, all other things in this world become insignificant in comparison. We need to recognize that God flows through our lives and continually allow Him to do so.

A man who was eventually martyred in Africa wrote the following words from a prison cell: "I'm part of the fellowship of the unashamed. The die has been cast. I've stepped over the line. The decision has been made. I am a disciple of Jesus Christ. I won't step back, let up, slow down, back away or be still. My past is redeemed, my present makes sense, my future is secure. I'm finished with low living and sight-walking and smooth knees, colorless dreams, worldly visions and tame talking, cheap giving and dwarfed goals. Now my face is set, my gait is fast. My goal is Heaven; my reward is awaiting me. My way may be rough. Sometimes my companions may be few. But my guide is reliable; my mission is clear. I won't give up or shut up or let up until I have stayed up and stood up and prayed up for the cause of Jesus Christ. I must go 'til He comes, give 'til I drop, preach and teach until everyone knows, work until He stops me and when He comes for His own, He will have no trouble recognizing me because my banner will have been set. I am a follower and disciple of Jesus Christ."

CHAPTER 12

FOLLOW THE LEADER
Ephesians 5:1-7

The first two verses of Ephesians 5 tell us how to follow the leader, and we are to do it by walking in love and as children. Verses 3-7 show us that we should follow the leader by living as saints.

The word *"dear"* in verse 1 is a very interesting word. There is a word that is translated in the New Testament as "dear" that means "honor" or "prize," but this is not that word. Instead, it is a word that has its root in the Greek word *agape*, so it refers to loving children. The word "children" there expresses the idea that we are begotten into the family of God.

The Bible has much to say about how God loves us.

John 15:13 says, *"Greater love hath no man than this, that a man lay down his life for his friends."*

Romans 5:8 says, *"But God commendeth his love toward us, in that, while we were yet sinners, Christ died for us."*

When we think about being followers of God, what we really should be doing is striving to be imitators of God. We do this by walking in love as Christ loved us, according to verse 2 of Ephesians 5.

The second half of verse 3 refers to the Old Testament practice of offering sacrifices to God. In the Old Testament the burnt offering was the highest expression of love to God. It was one of three that were called "savor" offerings.

There were varying degrees of these offerings. For instance, you could bring anything from a turtledove to a full-grown bull as an offering. The size of the offering was an indication of your love and appreciation for God. That is why when telling us in verse 2 to *"walk in love,"* Paul uses the burnt offering as an illustration.

This is a charge to radical love. It is a love that you and I are not used to and do not understand, much like the love of God that was described in the closing verses of Ephesians 3.

The latter chapters of Ephesians, however, talk more about relationships. The final verses of Ephesians 5 discuss marriage relationships and the importance of a married life, and the opening verses of Ephesians 6 refer to parent-child relationships as well as those between employer and employee. In all of these situations, we are instructed to walk in love as His children.

A key part of this chapter is the phrase *"given himself for us"* in verse 2. How much does God love you? If you ever doubt for a moment His love for you, stop and think back to what He did for you at the cross.

Look at Eph. 5:25. *"Husbands, love your wives, even as Christ also loved the church, and gave himself for it."*

The Bible says a lot about husbands and wives. When a married couple comes in to talk with me, the wife is usually very loving, even if the husband is not. The book of Titus says that the wife is to learn to love her husband from the example and teaching of the elderly women. But there never seems to be a command in the New Testament for wives to love their husbands, although men are commanded to love their wives. The verse that gives this commandment speaks of a love unto death.

We know Christ loves us because He gave His life for us. Wives are to know their husbands' love because it should have a depth far beyond what we normally consider men and women to give of each other.

When you accept Jesus Christ as your Saviour, you do it one time. But if you are going to choose to love God and the significant people in your life, it must be a daily choice that you make.

My wife and I have four children, all of whom are now in their 20s and 30s. Back when we only had our two oldest children, our daughter was asked to be in a wedding. She was about four years old, and she was very excited about this opportunity. In fact, she talked constantly about this wedding ceremony she was participating in.

One day I came home and had some time in the afternoon, so I said, "JoAnna, would you like to play a game?"

"Yes," she said. "I'd like to play 'wedding.'"

We went into the living room and, of course, she wanted to be the bride. I thought she would want to marry me, but she said, "You're going to be the preacher." There was no one for her to marry.

My son Jonathan, who was two years old at the time, walked into the house carrying cars and trucks, covered in dirt from head to toe from playing outside. "I'll marry Jonathan," said JoAnna.

So we had the wedding right there in the living room. I started going through the wedding vows, looking at Jonathan and reciting the usual "do you take this woman, from this day forward, etc." While he had never been to a wedding in his life, he soon realized that whatever was going on here with his sister was something he wanted no part of.

"No!" he shouted, pulling his arm away and running out the door. That was his decision.

If you are going to follow the leader in your marriage and with regard to your children, your work or any other aspect of your life, you have to realize that it is a decision you must make every day of your life. There are all kinds of enemies that surround us and try to take us away from following Him.

When we talk about walking in love as it is mentioned in these passages, there are several kinds of love to consider. There is a sacrificial love that is even unto death. There is a suffering love that must face the many injustices, cruelties and disappointments of life. There is an intercessory love that Christ shows toward us when He goes before the Father on our behalf.

There is a sanctifying love, as we see in verse 26. *"That he might sanctify and cleanse it with the washing of water by the word."*

Is your spouse more like Christ because of you? Are the people who are important in your life becoming more like Christ in any way because of your influence?

This love is also a love through which we give ourselves over to others. Many years ago, Dr. Robert McQuilken, the president of Columbia Bible College, suddenly resigned. Here is what he wrote for that occasion: "My dear wife Muriel has been in failing mental health for about eight years. So far I have been able to carry both her ever-growing needs and my leadership responsibilities here at the college. But recently it has become apparent that she is contented most of the time I am with her and almost none of the time I am away from her. It is not just discontent; she is filled with fear, even terror. When I leave home she thinks she has lost me and always goes in search of me, then sometimes becomes angry when she cannot reach me. So it has become clear to me that she needs me full-time. This decision, in a way, was made 42 years ago when I made a promise to care for Muriel in sickness and in health 'til in death we do part. Thus, integrity and keeping my word has something to do with this decision, but so does fairness. She has faithfully cared for me all these years, and if I care for her the next 40 I will not be out of her debt. Duty, however, can be grim and stoic. But there is more. I love Muriel. Her childlike dependence on me, her confidence in me, her warm love, the occasional flashes of that wit I used to relish, her happy spirit and tough and resilience in the face of continuing stress and frustration – because of this, I do not have to take care of her, but I get to take care of her. It is a high honor to care for so wonderful a person."

If you are married, think of it like a triangle. You are the one of the bottom corners, your spouse is the other, and the Lord is the third corner above you. The closer you and your spouse get toward the Lord, the closer you get to each other.

When He tells us to walk in love, He is saying, "Walk as if you were a child." You remember that child of yours who would do anything you asked, then one day said no when you asked for something. "What happened to my wonderful child?" you asked yourself. God is asking you and me to live like a child in following Him.

The second thing He says is in verses 3-7, and that is to live like a saint. Before we look at this passage, let's consider a number of things going on in our society today.

In 1880, according to historian Robert Griswald, one couple out of every 21 divorced in this country – fewer than five percent. By 1991, that number rose to 47 percent. In 2005, according to U.S. Census Bureau statistics, the divorce rate fell to 38 percent, but the drop is partly due to the fact that more couples are living together without being married.

In fact, according to statistics, the best age to get married and stay married is the age of 60. But most of us cannot wait until 60 to get married.

If you have been through the agony of a divorce, let me encourage you to begin right now, wherever you are, living as a saint. Whatever your married life may be like at this time, live like a saint.

Let me give you six habits of happily married couples. This list is not original with me, but these points are very good ones.

First, give each other pleasure. Ask yourself in every situation, "Will this cause pain or pleasure?"

I spoke at a men's retreat in the Florida Keys recently for my good friend, pastor Tony Hammon. He called me and told me that after I spoke at the Friday night meeting, I could go fishing with the group Saturday morning or bring my wife with me and spend the day with her. Now I love to fish, so you can see the dilemma this presented. I wondered whether I should even tell my wife about this.

When I told her, she said that she would like to go down and spend that time with me. So we did, and we had a ball. I couldn't have cared less about fishing, but there was a temptation because of my love for fishing.

Second, create mutually satisfying love and friendship rituals. Spend time together as a couple. Don't you ever wish the kids would go do something on their own? Don't you wish the cell phone would just quit ringing? Shut it off.

Third, discuss issues openly and honestly in a safe environment. If you are married, you must be willing to talk about the tough issues in your relationship and do it in a safe way.

Fourth, use good communication skills to resolve hot issues. Maybe you don't have any hot issues right now, but you will. One of the greatest sciences of communication is learning to listen.

I have been preaching for nearly 40 years. Recently I have discovered that sometimes when I am preaching, I think I know what I said, only to discover that I did not say what I thought I said. When that happens, how is anyone supposed to understand what I'm talking about?

This happens in marriages and in other situations all the time. You talk to someone and you think they understand what you are saying, but as you continue the discussion you realize that they missed the point completely. The word "communication" comes from *communo*, which means "coming together as one." It suggests that when we communicate, we establish unity.

Fifth, grow close emotionally. If you are single and looking for someone to marry, you should desire someone you will spend the rest of your life with, someone you can share your heart with and have shared meaning. What are your vacation plans? What are your future educational plans? These major events should be pursued together. If you are married today, be thankful that God brought that special person into your life.

When John wrote the book of Revelation, he wrote to the church at Ephesus that its members were leaving their first love. I have often thought during this study of Ephesians that the city of Ephesus was much like south Florida, where I live. This part of the United States is a beautiful place to live, but there are many challenges here. It was the same in Ephesus.

Verses 3 and 5 refer to several sexual challenges. The word *"fornication"* in verse 3 is from *pornea*, a narrow term that speaks of sexual activity among the unmarried. *"Uncleanness"* refers to unclean thinking and vulgarity.

It is interesting that covetousness is mentioned in the same phrase. Paul is writing about coveting fornication or coveting uncleanness, and he says not to ever get involved in any of that.

These types of things are everywhere in our society today. If you want pornography, you can get it. It is not difficult to become involved in an illicit relationship if you really want to. But we are warned in these verses that those who participate in these activities will lose the blessing of God and the anointing of God.

Look at verse 5: *"For this ye know, that no whoremonger, nor unclean person, nor covetous man, who is an idolater, hath any inheritance in the kingdom of Christ and of God."* In this verse, an *"idolater"* is someone who worships the flesh. At the Judgment Seat of Christ, those who are guilty of these sins will lose what God has promised to them.

There is also a sensual challenge, as illustrated in verses 4 and 6. In verse 4, *"filthiness"* refers to vulgarity or obscenities and *"foolish talking"* includes what we get our word "moron" from. *"Jesting"* in this verse refers to dirty jokes. Paul writes at the end of verse 4 that we should prefer to give thanks rather than participate in this kind of communication.

In issuing these sexual and sensual challenges, God is encouraging us to follow the leader. Sometimes in life our path strays off-course, and we are urged to get back on track and follow Him. We all know how serious these challenges are. So many homes and relationships are not where they should be.

If you are in a relationship you should not be in, if you are having thoughts you should not be having, or if you are looking at things you should not be looking at, the only solution is repentance to God. Not only are you damaging your relationship with Him, but the blessings He wants to bestow upon you and the anointing He wants you to have in your life are not going to happen.

The word *"deceive"* is prominent in verse 6, as it was in verses 14 and 22 of Ephesians 4. The deceit mentioned in these verses is what causes us to stray from the path we should be on and wander off-course.

Look at verse 7. *"Be not ye therefore partakers with them."* The root word for *"partakers"* there refers to having something in common; it is the same word we get our word "fellowship" from. The Lord is telling us in these verses not to follow anyone down the wrong road, and if we do we bring the wrath of God upon us, as indicated in verse 6.

The type of wrath mentioned here is different from that in verse 31 of chapter 4, which in the Greek word *thumas* that suggests hot passion (also found in Eph. 6 when we are instructed not to provoke our children to anger). In this passage, however, it speaks of a wrath that leads to the blessings of God being taken from us because of these actions that He has forbidden.

We need to hear and be reminded from our pulpits of this kind of truth today. Any of us can easily fall into sin. We get embarrassed or hurt, we run from church, we run from God and those who love us, and we blame other people for what is happening. The only way back is through repentance. There is no other way.

The other challenge in these verses is a gratitude challenge, where we are instructed to give thanks. The phrase *"giving of thanks"* at the end of verse 4 includes the Greek word we get "eucharist" from and speaks of the overwhelming joy that God gives to us. What are you thankful for today?

Every Sunday morning when I leave my home early for the first service at our Broward campus, I stop by that "holy land" known as Starbucks for a cup of coffee. One morning I reached out at the drive-thru window to pay for my coffee, and the man serving me, who is a member of our church, said, "It's good to see you, Pastor. This one is on me." I was thankful for his kind gesture (and I wondered why I didn't order a few more items).

The tragic events at Virginia Tech in the spring of 2007, when a student took the lives of more than 30 other students before turning his gun on himself, were difficult to look at. I had trouble watching the news reports. There's been too much of that kind of violence in recent years. Here is what a Time magazine article said about some of the victims:

Like all college freshmen, Mary Karen Read was just starting out. She was thinking about joining a sorority and hoped to teach young children someday. She died in Norris Hall, during French class.

Another freshman, Reema Samaha, was an accomplished dancer who attended the same Virginia high school as the gunman.

So did Erin Peterson, a freshman who was majoring in international relations.

Daniel Perez Cueva, also an international-relations major, moved to the U.S. from Peru in 2002.

Matthew La Porte was on an ROTC scholarship and aspired to a career in the Air Force.

Ryan Clark played in the marching band and hoped to pursue a Ph.D. in neuroscience.

G.V. Loganathan, a native of India, was a professor at Virginia Tech for 25 years.

Kevin Granata was an expert in biomechanics and the father of three teenage children.

Brian Bluhm was pursuing a master's degree in water resources.

Jarrett Lane was a senior majoring in civil engineering.

Freshman Austin Cloyd planned to study international relations.

Henry Lee, another freshman, couldn't speak English when his family moved to the U.S. from China but ended up his high school's salutatorian.

Aeronautical-engineering professor Liviu Librescu survived the Holocaust as a child; students said that during Monday's shooting, he blocked the door to his classroom so they could flee.

Ross Alameddine loved music and was majoring in English.

Emily Hilscher was on the equestrian team and wanted to become a veterinarian.

Nicole White studied international relations and spent summers as a lifeguard at the YMCA.

Julia Pryde's graduate work on water purification took her to Ecuador and Peru.

The MySpace page for freshman Lauren McCain, who was majoring in international studies and German, said her two heroes were her brother and Jesus.

Civil-engineering graduate student Partahi Lumbantoruan hailed from Medan, Indonesia.

Jamie Bishop, a Fulbright scholar, had taught German at Tech since 2005.

Engineering graduate student Jeremy Herbstritt was voted Most Talkative by his high school class.

Rachael Hill was a standout high school volleyball player.

Caitlin Hammaren, a National Honor Society member, said she planned to go to law school.

Senior Maxine Turner was a month away from a degree in engineering.

Jocelyne Couture-Nowak taught French at the university for eight years. She had two daughters.

Leslie Sherman, a sophomore, was an avid student of history.

Puerto Rico native Juan Ortiz moved to Virginia with his wife last year to pursue a master's in engineering.

Daniel O'Neil enrolled in graduate school at Tech last fall. A high school classmate said, "He probably would have gone really far in life."

Every one of these people died that fateful day on the Virginia Tech campus. But the only question that really matters now is, "Where did they go?"

When we look at a chapter in the Word of God like Ephesians 5, we need to stop and ask ourselves, "What am I thankful for?" God speaks here about gratitude, about caring, about what is really important.

Are you glad that you're a child of God? Are you glad that He lives in your heart today? Are you glad that there are people in your life who care about you?

Each of us must make a conscious decision every day to accept the gratitude challenge. If you are saved, you are royalty. Because of that, and because of what He has done for you, you should walk like a child, live like a saint, and be an imitator of God.

CHAPTER 13

ORDERING YOUR PRIVATE LIFE
Ephesians 5:8-14

_____ లు సు _____

A s we look at the portions of Scripture being covered in this chapter, we need to consider a few things.

It is important to understand that it is easy to try to make a list of things that (we think) make up to be the Christian life. You might believe that because you do this or don't do that, you have a handle on the Christian life. There are a number of DOs and DON'Ts in these passages, and you can often find yourself thinking that you are accumulating "brownie points" with God by doing or not doing certain things. But we miss out on what the Bible is teaching us here, and it is vitally important to understand that you and I cannot do anything in our lives that is really effective in our Christian walk unless we do it in the power of the Holy Spirit of God.

When you accepted Jesus Christ into your life as your Saviour, at the moment the Holy Spirit came to live inside you. As He lives within you, He is moving and working in your life. It is easy for all of us to say, "I wish ..." or "Why can't they ..." about other people when it is a fact that the Holy Spirit must be working in my own life and I am accountable to God for myself. The things we have discussed from the book of Ephesians will likely be meaningless if they are not taken in that context.

Now that we are ready to talk about ordering our private lives, we need more than ever to understand the necessity of having the

Holy Spirit work in our lives. Each of you reading this should stop for a moment and say aloud, "I need the Holy Spirit at work in my life." It is too easy to think about your spouse, your children, your friends, or people at your place of employment that need to heed what we are studying. Get your mind off other people and get it on what you need.

Many of you probably have books from the "For Dummies" series in your library at home. My wife bought a copy of "Home Repair For Dummies," brought it home and gave it to me. There are scores of topics in this series.

When I first saw those books for sale, I thought they would never go anywhere because no one wants to think of himself as a dummy. But they are selling all over the place, and some experts believe that success is due partly to the fact that it takes the intimidation out of the learning process. What I want to do right now is take the intimidation out of this study, so that normal men and women can get a hold of this idea of ordering your private life.

The first thing to notice in Eph. 5:8-14 is the use of the personal pronoun *"ye"* or *"you"* in verse 8. God is talking about us individually. He is talking directly to you and to me. As far as I'm concerned, He is not talking about my wife or children or parents or friends or anyone else, but only to me.

There are two key words to understanding this passage. The first word is *"light."* It is used five times in these verses, and each time it is talking about giving light, but the last time in verse 14 it is a Greek word that literally means "to shine forth the light." If you and I are living according to these verses, we are shining forth that light to the world.

The other word is *"darkness."* It means to deprive of light. God is saying that in ordering your private life, you need to know what is dark and bring it to light so that when you go out in public you can shine forth the light. These verses speak of the contrast between darkness and light.

You will recall that verse 1 of chapter 5 tells us to be imitators of God and follow Him as children. Now we are seeing how that command extends to our private lives.

To break down this passage a little more, verse 8-9 focus on our **daily routines**, verses 10-11 talk about our **daily recognition** of God living within us, verses 12-13 speak of our **daily repentance** and walk with God, and in verse 14 is the idea of **daily renewal**.

How can I order my life in my daily routine? Look at verse 8. *"For ye were sometimes darkness, but now are ye light in the Lord: walk as children of light."* Reputation is what other people know and think about us. Character is what we know about ourselves and what God knows about us. There is a big difference between reputation and character.

With this in mind, continue to verse 9: *"For the fruit of the Spirit is in all goodness and righteousness and truth."* In this verse, *"goodness"* refers to character, *"righteousness"* is without partiality or prejudice, and *"truth"* is unconcealed.

At our Christian school, the faculty is filled with people who are experts at the subjects they teach but what matters even more to them, as well as many of our students and their parents, is their character.

I can stand in a pulpit and preach to a congregation of people about how they should live, and I can cite dozens of Bible verses to back up my arguments, but what really matters is the way I conduct myself in my private life because that is what makes up my character.

Each of us knows what we are really like inside. It takes discipline to build character and order our private lives. We like gratification, and for things to always come our way, but we all need to have discipline in various areas of life.

If you see a runner, especially a distance runner, who is victorious in a race, you know that he has trained hard and endured pain to get to that point. It takes time to do that; it doesn't happen overnight.

Many people, after only a few months of marriage, say, "I can't believe the problems we're having." Welcome to the club. Everyone has problems, and no married couple is immune from that. The same goes for the workplace. You're not going to be on the job very long in one place without a few problems.

To build character, you have to go through pain. In his book "The Road Less Traveled," Scott Peck wrote these words: "Daily gratification is a process of scheduling the pain and pleasures of life in such a way as to be able to go through the pleasure by meeting and experiencing the pain first and getting it over with."

You see a great piece of cake with phenomenal frosting on the top. Maybe you like to go to the frosting first, like I have done at times, because it looks so good. In life, we always want the frosting without having to deal with the less-desirable portions. But the way you deal with pain determines the character you will have in your life.

Recently I was at a silent auction for one of our Christian schools. I like to sign up for items and hope that other people will come in and outbid me, because I want to drive the price up to the benefit of the school. I saw a huge picture and signed my name on the sheet next to it, thinking that many others would come behind me.

Imagine my surprise when I was the high bidder. It is beautiful, but it is a gigantic picture. I was exhausted after my son-in-law and I carried it to the car that night. I wondered what I would tell my wife when I got home. Maybe we would give it away as a Christmas gift, I thought.

I was surprised once more when I got home and my wife said, "I like this picture." I could tell by the look on her face that she really liked it. So where would we hang it? The only option at first seemed to be buying a new house, but we couldn't afford that.

My wife decided that we would repaint the great room and family room because of this new picture. I thought, "Why did I have to buy this picture?"

I bought a lot of paint, and my three sons spent several days getting those two rooms painted. It was a lot of work and expense, but now when you visit our home you can enjoy this beautiful picture. When I look at it, I will always think a little bit about what we went through to get it on the wall.

Everything in life has pain. Many of you reading this right now have some kind of pain in your life. To build character takes discipline, and discipline comes by dealing with pain and endurance.

Look at Phil. 3:13-14. *"Brethren, I count not myself to have apprehended: but this one thing I do, forgetting those things which are behind, and reaching forth unto those things which are before,*

I press toward the mark for the prize of the high calling of God in Christ Jesus."

Another way of putting it can be found in James 1:12. *"Blessed is the man that endureth temptation: for when he is tried, he shall receive the crown of life, which the Lord hath promised to them that love him."*

Look back at your life. Are there times when you wish you had not quit? Maybe it was in high school or college. You might think about a former teacher you had and wish you had become a teacher. Maybe there was a situation in your marriage where you just quit.

There are always times of transition, but it's never good to quit. Some good advice is, "You build endurance by learning how to crash through the quitting points."

The Bible says in Jer. 29:13-14, *"And ye shall seek me, and find me, when ye shall search for me with all your heart. And I will be found of you, saith the LORD: and I will turn away your captivity, and I will gather you from all the nations, and from all the places whither I have driven you, saith the LORD; and I will bring you again into the place whence I caused you to be carried away captive."*

God is saying here that in all of our lives there are points where, if we are not careful, we will run into breaking points, but He wants us to be faithful in what He has called us to do. You may be facing such a decision in your life right now. But if you quit this time, then it will be easier to quit the next time around. After a while you will become known, at least in your own heart, as a quitter.

Sometimes you might not even want to go to God in prayer because you think of so many failures in your life. Aren't you glad God is so quick to forgive us?

Building character not only takes discipline and endurance, it also takes love, like the love mentioned in Eph. 4:32. *"And be ye kind one to another, tenderhearted, forgiving one another, even as God for Christ's sake hath forgiven you."*

When you see another person and the burdens he or she may be carrying, it's important to think about this: "I wonder what it's like to walk a mile in that person's shoes."

If you are healthy, think about how it would feel to be handicapped. If you are working, think about how it would feel to be unemployed. You might not have any trouble making your mortgage payments right now, but there are plenty of people who don't know where that money will be coming from in the next month. If you are happily married, what would it be like to be in the shoes of that person who is divorced?

As you have your private time with God, you will begin to learn that He tenderly loves you. Here is a portion of what the Bible says about that.

"Since thou wast precious in my sight, thou hast been honourable, and I have loved thee." (Is. 43:4)

"Like as a father pitieth his children, so the LORD pitieth them that fear him." (Ps. 103:13)

But in addition to tender love, we learn tough love. There will always be situations in character building when we need tough love. There is no such thing as "peace at any cost."

Sometimes as a husband or wife, or in your place of employment, or some other situation, you need tough love.

Many of you remember President Ronald Reagan's speech June 12, 1987, at the Brandenburg Gate in West Berlin, when he said, "Mr. Gorbachev, tear down this wall." He was talking about giving freedom to people who needed it. That was tough love.

There are times when you must sit down and confront someone. How do you do it? Gal. 6:1 tells us how. *"Brethren, if a man be overtaken in a fault, ye which are spiritual, restore such an one in the spirit of meekness; considering thyself, lest thou also be tempted."*

Pay particular attention to the word *"restore."* The Bible doesn't say that you are to give that person a piece of your mind or really let him have it. This verse explains that you must be *"spiritual,"* meaning that you must ask God to cleanse you and fill you so that you can do what you must do in the right way, with the goal always being restoration.

One of the most difficult things in life to do is to practice tough love in a Biblical way, but it is a part of ordering your private life.

The Bible also speaks about sacrificial love. Every marriage will have its struggles that go on for a while, but let me encourage you to out love, out bless and out serve your partner, being all that you can be in your marriage. You might think you can't do that, but you can do it in the Lord.

In the Old Testament, when David was going through a difficult time in his life, as people were trying to overthrow his government, he didn't think he could take any more and he felt like throwing in the towel. But the Bible says in I Sam. 30:6 that he *"encouraged himself in the LORD his God."*

Psalm 46:1 says, *"God is our refuge and strength, a very present help in trouble."* That is the kind of God that we serve today.

Ordering our private life also deals with our daily recognition and awareness. Look at Eph. 5:10-11. "Proving what is acceptable unto the Lord. And have no fellowship with the unfruitful works of darkness, but rather reprove them."

It doesn't matter what we think; it's what God finds acceptable that counts. We must shine His light on the darkness in our lives and expose it. That is what these verses are talking about.

Verse 12 says, *"For it is a shame even to speak of those things which are done of them in secret."* The biggest problem for nearly all of us is gossip. Don't we like it at least a little bit? Of course we do; it makes us feel good. It makes us feel better than the people we're talking about.

Whenever I'm thinking in a negative way about someone else, it makes me feel a little better about myself. The problem with that type of thinking is that my self-worth is based on comparison with others, when in reality my self-worth should come from Him and what He has given to me.

When you are a child of God, you are a member of royalty. The Bible says in Rom. 8:16-17, "The Spirit itself beareth witness with our spirit, that we are the children of God: And if children, then heirs; heirs of God, and joint-heirs with Christ; if so be that we suffer with him, that we may be also glorified together."

There are many more examples of this. Here are two:

"Who hath also sealed us, and given the earnest of the Spirit in our hearts." (II Cor. 1:22)

"In whom ye also trusted, after that ye heard the word of truth, the gospel of your salvation: in whom also after that ye believed, ye were sealed with that holy Spirit of promise, Which is the earnest of

our inheritance until the redemption of the purchased possession, unto the praise of his glory." (Eph. 1:13-14)

The Bible goes on and on with verses that tell us our confidence is in Him, and we share in the estate of what God has given to us, so He is changing us regularly. As we start out at the beginning of each new day, we can say to one another, "God is in charge of what I'm all about and working in my life today." That is the recognition of the awareness of God.

Back in Ephesians 5, verses 12-13 also speak about daily repentance. "For it is a shame even to speak of those things which are done of them in secret. But all things that are reproved are made manifest by the light: for whatsoever doth make manifest is light."

What has been done in the dark is best kept in the dark. If you have some deep, dark secrets about your life that you are hiding from everyone else, the best thing you can do is give them to God, ask Him for the victory, and don't let the light bring them forth.

The Holy Spirit knows exactly what He is doing in our hearts and lives, and you cannot hide things from God. The Expositors Bible Commentary puts it this way: "Evil can no longer masquerade as anything else but evil."

Carl Meninger, a medical doctor, wrote a book in the 1970s entitled "Whatever Happened to Sin?" He told a fascinating story about a man in Chicago who was probably deranged. This man would go out onto the busy streets of Chicago, raise his hand high in the air, point at people walking by and shout, "Guilty!"

Some people would look at the man and wonder when the men in white coats were coming to take him away. But often he would shout at people who had just done something wrong. One man later said that he had just left a liaison with a woman who was not his wife, and this stranger proclaimed, "Guilty!" as he walked by. Another man who had embezzled money from his company gave the same report.

When you have the Holy Spirit of God in your life, you know what He is telling you. It is better to ask God for help with your struggle in privacy of your time alone with Him. He certainly understands; He *"was in all points tempted like as we are, yet without sin."* (Heb. 4:15)

It's better to say, "God, I know you understand what I am going through, and I recognize it as well," and let Him do a work in your life.

Look at verse 14. *"Wherefore he saith, Awake thou that sleepest, and arise from the dead, and Christ shall give thee light."*

Many believe that this was actually a hymn sung by the early church during a believer's baptism. This verse talks about how a person's conviction makes him or her alive to God.

Of all people, Christians should shine forth the light of what people in this world need, because Jesus is the Light of the world. The message to Christians in verse 14 is, "Wake up! You've got what you need, so wake up and live for Him; understand who He is."

An old song goes, "It's me, it's me, it's me, oh Lord, standing in need of prayer." We must get our eyes off everything and everyone else. It's easy to talk about what is wrong in Washington, in our state or local community, or where we work. But God is saying, "Wake up. Look at yourself." The problem with me is me. I have a hard enough time keeping myself straight.

I want to make a challenge to you right now. II Chr. 7:14 says, "If my people, which are called by my name, shall humble themselves, and pray, and seek my face, and turn from their wicked ways; then will I hear from heaven, and will forgive their sin, and will heal their land." People ask me all the time, "What's going to happen when so-and-so is elected president? What are we going to do?"

When we look at where we live, the bottom line is that we as believers are of another kingdom and another world. That doesn't mean that we shut our eyes and pretend this world doesn't matter. But all of us before God need to order our private lives, because when you stand before God you will be accountable for yourself.

We can all tell other people what is wrong with our spouses or our children, and the children can tell people what is wrong with their parents. When a couple sits down to discuss their marriage and attempts to be transparent about each other's problems, one person invariably will say, "I'm not that bad." Yes, you are – not in our eyes, but before Him.

We are what we are by the grace of God. Aren't you glad about that? Only through the Holy Spirit working in us can we get to where we need to be.

CHAPTER 14

MORE THAN WORDS
Ephesians 5:15-17

—⟋⟍⟋⟍—

I think Christianity, in some sense, is obsessed with words. Sometimes I ask myself the question, "Is Christianity more than words?"

We come to church and we hear preachers and teachers use words. We sing songs of worship that contain words. We print bulletins filled with words. Of course, our Bibles also contain thousands of words.

After the recent graduation ceremonies at our Christian school, I reflected upon my own education and realized that I have spent a lot of time studying words – reading books, memorizing facts, taking tests and reciting various passages filled with words.

Too often we find ourselves believing that the Christian life is all about having the right words to say. While that may be true to a certain extent, and there are specific words for us to build our lives around, we must ask ourselves if there is more to the Christian life than that.

It is interesting to note that in the first three chapters of Ephesians there are no commands, because those chapters were written to tell the people of Ephesus who they are and what God has made them to be. Beginning in chapter 4, God is essentially saying, "All right, because you are this, I will give you these commands."

Ephesus was a key city in the Roman empire, and it was full of spiritual warfare. Paul spent an extraordinary amount of time there – two full years, which was a long time for him to stay in one place with a church.

Amid this spiritual warfare, some miraculous things happened in Ephesus during Paul's ministry. Acts 19:12 says, "So that from his body were brought unto the sick handkerchiefs or aprons, and the diseases departed from them, and the evil spirits went out of them."

This is amazing. When Paul merely touched pieces of cloth or garments, people would grab them and take them to sick people, and those who touched them were healed of their sicknesses.

Ephesus was a city of great spirituality, both good and bad. God was doing a great work there, but Paul was working in a place full of pagan spirituality. The enormous temple of Artemus, considered one of the seven wonders of the ancient world, was in Ephesus and all sorts of evil practices went on there.

In fact, Acts 19 recounts the story of seven sons of a Jewish priest who became followers of Christ and their encounter with a demon-possessed man. They tried to cast out the demon, but the possessed man overpowered all seven of them. He beat them all up and tore off their clothes, so that they ran from the fight bleeding and naked. The spiritual warfare in Ephesus was that intense.

Acts 19 also talks about a riot in the city. A man named Demetrius made his living manufacturing idols for people to buy, take home and worship. When Paul came to town preaching about the one true God, Demetrius saw a huge drop in business as people realized he was making false gods. This made him very upset.

Demetrius started a riot among the people of Ephesus. "Do you see what this evil man Paul is doing?" he said. "He is destroying our community and our culture."

So as these people were rioting in a large theater, Paul wanted to go there and talk to this group that might try to kill him. Fortunately, nothing like that happened. Paul's disciples convinced him to go somewhere else, and cooler heads prevailed in the theater. Someone stood in the theater and addressed the people, telling them that this was not the way to resolve these issues. Either Paul's words would be proven true, they decided, or they wouldn't.

But one can see from this incident how much power the forces of evil had in Ephesus at this time. The fastest-growing cult at the time of Paul's New Testament writings was imperial worship. The emperors of the Roman empire took on divine names. Titles like "Lord," "Saviour," or "He who brings hope and peace" – attributes we would ascribe to God – were taken on by these rulers for their own use. It was common in the first century to hear someone say, "There is no lord but Caesar." If you said that Jesus is lord, that was in direct contradiction to what Caesar said and his people were taught to believe. The practice of worshipping these emperors was growing at a rapid rate during this time.

As we saw a few pages ago, Paul expressed repeatedly in Ephesians 5 that we are to be light and that light exposes what was in darkness. "The truth will come through," he was saying. These writings were composed in the context of great pagan spirituality that was so common in the region during his ministry. It was a very dark world.

Paul told the Ephesian believers, "You have the Spirit of God in you. Somehow the light will shine through you." We can relate to this, because we live in a time that in many ways is very evil. As Christians, we are charged with transforming this world. How can we do that?

Look at Eph. 5:15-17. *"See then that ye walk circumspectly, not as fools, but as wise, Redeeming the time, because the days are evil. Wherefore be ye not unwise, but understanding what the will of the Lord is."*

We assume so much in Christianity. We think that we could do so much if we only had the right words to say.

During my undergraduate studies I minored in youth ministries and had the same professor for several of those classes. One verse he came back to over and over again was I Thess. 2:8. *"So being affectionately desirous of you, we were willing to have imparted unto you, not the gospel of God only, but also our own souls, because ye were dear unto us."*

My professor was fond of saying, "Your ministry starts with a closing prayer." What he meant was that most young people were not going to remember what I said. It's what I do after I stop talking that matters the most.

I am often approached by a young person who has a burden for a friend to be saved and know God. This is the most common question I hear: "Pastor, will you talk to my friend for me?" Part of me wants to immediately say, "Yes, I would love to share the Gospel with your friend." But another side of me is hesitant, and I often ask, "Why do you want me to do it?"

Almost without exception, the answer is, "Because you can say it so much better than I can. You have the right words." It's as if there are these magic words to say that will cause someone to instantly want to be converted.

Sometimes a young person will bring a friend up and say, "Pastor, tell him about God." They think that I'm just going to explain a few things in five minutes, and this person's life will be totally changed, and he'll be on the floor crying out to God.

But Paul's challenge in I Thess. 2:8 emphasizes that it's not just by giving the "right" words, but by sharing our lives that we make an impact. It's by sharing ourselves with people that we are effective in sharing the Gospel.

A youth pastor once said, "When I recall the adults in my life who have shown me love, I don't remember anything they ever said to me. I just remember that when we were together, one way or another, they paid attention to me. Those memories of God and adults sustain me even to this day."

I can ask some of the teens in our church's youth group what they remember about the messages they've heard the past few years. As much as I wish they would say, "Oh, that Sunday night in October of 2002, you used these five points," and recite my outline from that sermon, that never happens. I'm more likely to hear, "Well, I don't know, maybe it was that time you said such-and-such," and they stammer through something they really don't remember.

Think about the sermon you heard last Sunday morning. You might remember a particular story or illustration, but out of the 30 minutes or more your pastor spoke, you will not remember much of what he said.

But what you will always remember, whether as a member of a youth group or an adult in a church congregation, was that trip you took with your youth leader or the time you had dinner with your pastor at a favorite restaurant. People don't remember the words that were said from the pulpit as much as they do the lives that were shared with them.

In our churches today, Christianity has become all about activity and all about words. In fact, Sunday can become the most stressful day of the week.

Think about it. You get up early and have to get dressed so you look nice. If you have kids, that task has just doubled or tripled. A toddler does not always want to get up and comb her hair and put on fancy clothes, no matter what day of the week it is. Watching television in her pajamas can be very appealing.

Meanwhile, you run around the house trying to find socks that match and a decent-looking tie, or a dress that isn't wrinkled. By the time everyone is dressed and in the car, you might already be screaming at each other. But once you arrive at church, your demeanor instantly changes and you greet everyone with, "Good morning. How are you? Oh, I'm great. I'm blessed. Praise the Lord."

So you keep that happy face plastered on your head all morning long, while in the back of your mind you consider how you're going to let your son or daughter have it because of what they did earlier that morning. When I was a kid, Sunday afternoons were always trouble for me because I usually had done something wrong that morning, and when we got back home Mom and Dad would nail me for it.

But we think that we can just say the right words and no one will notice how things really are. We get so caught up in our words that we forget to just be who we are.

When was the last time you were just quiet, sitting still with no distractions? I'm talking about just sitting down and saying, "Lord, for the next 20 minutes I'm going to be quiet. I'm not going to read anything, recite some eloquent prayer or a list of things I want from

You. We can just sit together, and if I keep quiet, maybe I can hear You can say something to me."

With everything from cell phones to iPods strapped to our bodies, we live in a state of constant noise. We just need to get quiet for a while and shut out the noise.

So what would happen if our Christianity became more than just words?

First, we would finally be able to see. There is a story in Luke 7 about Jesus dining in a Pharisee's home, and it starts in verse 36: *"And one of the Pharisees desired him that he would eat with him. And he went into the Pharisee's house, and sat down to meat."*

In this culture, people often invited their friends over for dinner because they lived under what was called the Law of Reciprocity. If I invited a good friend over to my house for a meal, I know that he would have to invite me to his house the next week. That's the way it worked back then. So this Pharisee, knowing that Jesus had become an important person in the region, invited him over for dinner thinking that he would get the same offer in return.

Look at the next verse. "And, behold, a woman in the city, which was a sinner, when she knew that Jesus sat at meat in the Pharisee's house, brought an alabaster box of ointment."

Obviously, this is not the type of person normally seen at one of these functions. Who invites a prostitute over for dinner? In addition to that, there was a caste system in effect at this time and she was an outcast who had absolutely nothing to offer to anyone.

Verse 38 says that the woman *"stood at his feet behind him weeping, and began to wash his feet with tears, and did wipe them with the hairs of her head, and kissed his feet, and anointed them with the ointment."*

Of course, the Pharisee host was less than pleased at this woman's presence. Look at verse 39. *"Now when the Pharisee which had bidden him saw it, he spake within himself, saying, This man, if he were a prophet, would have known who and what manner of woman this is that toucheth him: for she is a sinner."*

This man was convinced that if Jesus knew what she was, He would get away from her in a hurry. Isn't that what we do all the time? We constantly label people, saying, "He's this" or "She's that," and that label is the first thing that comes to mind whenever we see them.

At this writing, the presidential elections are about a year away but we are already deep into the debate process. It's common to ask people during this time, "Who are you going to vote for?" That question is often nothing more than an invitation to fight. If I find out that you and I are voting for opposite candidates, I will be prone to label you based on that, and you might tend to label me as well.

When the Pharisee labeled the sinful woman, Jesus responded by telling a story about a man who forgave two debts, one for 500 pence and the other for 50. Jesus asked who would be more thankful, and the obvious answer was the person who owed the greater amount. Then Jesus pointed out this woman's greater need of forgiveness in her own life and her gratefulness for it.

Finally, we see the words of Christ in verse 44. *"And he turned to the woman, and said unto Simon, Seest thou this woman? I entered into thine house, thou gavest me no water for my feet: but she hath washed my feet with tears, and wiped them with the hairs of her head."*

Jesus wanted the Pharisee to get past the words and the labels and see this woman for who she really was. We all need to start seeing people the way God sees them – in need of a Saviour.

When Christianity becomes more than just words, we are also finally able to hear. As we discussed earlier, you can hear a sermon today and you will probably remember about 10 percent of it next week.

Consider this quote from John Dobbenstein. "Christians, especially ministers, so often think that they must contribute something when in the presence of others. They often forget that listening can be a greater service than speaking."

When someone comes to me with a problem, my first impulse is to figure out the solution. But sometimes the person with the problem isn't looking for an answer from me. I have to remind myself that it might be better if I just sat down and listened for a little while. That may be all that is needed.

Franklin D. Roosevelt, the thirty-second President of the United States, reflected once upon the many times he stood at the end of a long receiving line at the White House. One after another, people would come by, shake his hand and say what an honor it was to meet him. He grew tired of this because of the robotic way in which people would exchange pleasantries, asking how someone was doing when they really didn't care. "No one is really listening to anything I say in these situations," he thought.

So he decided to conduct an experiment. At the next function, when greeted by someone, he said, "How are you today? I killed my mother-in-law this morning." To his amazement, these people would smile and say something nice before moving along in the line. They never even noticed the horrible thing he had said.

Finally the ambassador from Bolivia came by. Roosevelt greeted him with the same comment: "I killed my mother-in-law this morning." The ambassador looked at him, then pulled him close and said quietly, "Well, I'm sure she had it coming." At last, the president had found someone who actually listened to him.

Many times we encounter people who don't need fancy words or clever answers from us. They just need us to care enough about them to listen.

In Revelation 2 and 3, during a letter to one of the seven churches, John makes the same statement over and over again: *"He that hath an ear, let him hear what the Spirit says to the churches."* This was emphasized so often because John knew how people in the church are so likely to act first without listening, or we just say, "Yeah, yeah, OK," and go on our way. We have become so overcome with words and activity that we can't stop for five minutes and listen to something.

A study was conducted among teenage prostitutes in San Francisco, and the following question was asked: "What did you need the most, but not get, that contributed to you entering this lifestyle?" Almost every one of them said, "What I needed the most was for someone to listen to me – someone who cared enough to stop and listen to what I was going through."

Sometimes living out our faith in a dark world is more about listening than about talking. But if we are able to see and hear people for what they really are, I believe that we will be able to act with compassion toward them.

The story of the prodigal son in Luke 15 is probably familiar to everyone reading this. What I find fascinating about this is how the son, after spending his father's money and wasting so much of his life, returns home with this speech he has prepared for many miles and gone over a hundred times in his mind. Verse 21 says, *"And the son said unto him, Father, I have sinned against heaven, and in thy sight, and am no more worthy to be called thy son."*

But it's strange that the father seems to completely ignore what his son has worked so hard to say. He doesn't even say, "It's all right, son."

While the prodigal is pouring his heart out, the father's response is recorded in verses 22-24. *"But the father said to his servants, Bring forth the best robe, and put it on him; and put a ring on his hand, and shoes on his feet: And bring hither the fatted calf, and kill it; and let us eat, and be merry: For this my son was dead, and is alive again; he was lost, and is found."*

I don't know much about raising cattle, but I know that the meat from one cow will feed not just a family, but an entire village. There was no way to refrigerate meat in those days, so when the father ordered the fatted calf to be killed, you knew that there would be a lot of steaks consumed that day. It was a celebration for the whole town.

The son's words are unimportant because the father is filled with so much compassion toward him that it doesn't matter what is said. He saw his son for what he was, he heard him (although it didn't seem that way), and he was able to act with compassion.

Sometimes living out our faith consists of simply acting with compassion. People go on mission trips and often they never preach a stirring message or share some deep spiritual truth with another person. They might paint or build something, participating in a project that meets an important need in that community, whether in the United States or some other country. That can be much more of a light in a darkened world than anything we could ever say.

Back in Ephesians 5, look at verses 18-20. "And be not drunk with wine, wherein is excess; but be filled with the Spirit; Speaking to yourselves in psalms and hymns and spiritual songs, singing and making melody in your heart to the Lord; Giving thanks always for all things unto God and the Father in the name of our Lord Jesus Christ."

The harvest in that time was a great celebration. As you might imagine, people would stand in large vats and stomp grapes, with the juice flowing out of a small hole at the bottom of each vat into a container. That was a great time of joy and excitement, and everyone got together for the harvesting of the grapes. In fact, if someone were seen treading the grapes alone, it was seen as a sign of judgment or a sad occurrence.

Isaiah 65:8 says, *"Thus saith the LORD, As the new wine is found in the cluster, and one saith, Destroy it not; for a blessing is in it: so will I do for my servants' sakes, that I may not destroy them all."*

The grape juice and wine are part of God's good creation. Paul encourages us in Ephesians not to abuse it or let it control us; getting drunk on wine is an abuse of the good creation of God. The product of the grapes was to be used for a time of joy.

Because of this, we are to sing songs as described in verse 19. Our lives are to be such that if we are living as light in this world like we should, we will be a people that knows how to celebrate.

C.S. Lewis said, "Our Lord finds our desires not too strong but too weak. We are half-hearted creatures, fooling about with drink and sex and ambition, when infinite joy is offered to us. Like an ignorant child who wants to go on making mud pies in the slum because he cannot imagine what is meant by the offer of a holiday at sea, we are far too easily pleased."

What are you and your family known for in your neighborhood? Is your house known as a place of celebration? Your neighbors should say about you, "That Christian family across the street is always happy and having fun. There is something about them that always makes other people welcome there."

When did it become the norm for Christians to be known as the people who don't know how to have fun? When did joy and celebration become strange to us? We are far too easily pleased to understand the great joy that God has provided for us.

Oliver Wendell Holmes, the famed U.S. Supreme Court justice of more than three decades, said, "I might have entered the ministry if certain clergymen I knew had not looked and acted so much like undertakers."

Do others see us as people of great joy and love for everyone, who would invite the whole neighborhood over as the prodigal son's father did, to celebrate what God has given us?

We see in Luke 7:34 how many people saw Jesus. *"The Son of man is come eating and drinking; and ye say, Behold a gluttonous man, and a winebibber, a friend of publicans and sinners!"*

You know you are becoming more like Jesus when religious people stand on the outside and say, "That guy is a friend to sinners. He hangs out with some shady characters, and he loves and accepts them. There's something wrong with him." That's what the Pharisees said about Christ. They were the finger-pointers in the community.

Recently a youth group from our church went on a mission trip to help with hurricane relief in Mississippi. There was devastation like I had never seen in my life. As we helped rebuild homes and perform other similar tasks, young people in our group would say, "This is great, but when are we going to share the Gospel with people here and tell them about Jesus?"

I said, "That's a good question. But as we've been here working and helping these people, that has been our Gospel presentation. They are seeing Jesus through us."

Paul encouraged the Ephesians that, despite the pagan and evil influences in their city, they could be a light in the darkness that pointed others to the Gospel. We should do the same. The way to do that is by more than just words. It is by seeing and hearing people and acting with compassion toward them.

CHAPTER 15

FAMILY MATTERS
Ephesians 5:18-24

—⟨⟩⟨⟩—

It is important, when looking at a passage of Scripture, to consider the culture of the day in which it was written as well as what is happening today. With that in mind, think about our present culture in the area of family matters.

We are living in a society in which it is difficult to have a single family structure that is succinct and clear. For instance, in many of our homes both spouses work and the wife often earns more than the husband. That can sometimes be a cause for concern within a family.

Sometimes there are issues regarding trust in a marriage because one spouse or the other has been less than faithful in years past.

We hear a lot of talk today about marriage being an equal partnership. We are also living in a generation where the man of the house frequently has less of a leadership role in the family. On the other hand, many women are coming out of backgrounds where they were abused by men. Spouses on both sides are acknowledging that there is a great deal more stress in their lives than before.

We have a number of single parents in our church, raising their children alone. They are the heroes and heroines of our church in many ways because they are attempt to do by themselves what a husband, a wife, a father and a mother should do.

Sometimes men and women have jobs that require a lot of travel, and husbands and wives may not see each other except for a few hours on the weekend.

A major point of contention in many marriages is the question of who calls the shots where the money is concerned. Finances can be a great concern, especially in places like south Florida, where I live, because the cost of living is high.

As people work with other adults and learn about their families, they are exposed to various points of view in the area of rearing children. There can even be differing points of view within a single family on that subject.

Because of all of the messages that are bombarding us in society today, it can be hard to know what God would like to say to us regarding the family. There are some principles in the book of Ephesians that we all need to understand so that we can better establish our families the way God would have us do so.

Matthew Henry, a great theologian, wrote these words: "A woman was not made out of a man's head to top him, nor out of his feet to be trampled upon by him, but out of his side to be equal to him, under his arm to be protected, and near his heart to be loved."

Charles Shedd put it so well when he wrote, "Marriage is not so much about finding the right person as it is about being the right person."

There are some key words that we must understand when we think about family matters. Look at verse 21 of Ephesians 5. *"Submitting yourselves one to another in the fear of God."*

Often a man will say, "Wife, you are to submit to me. You are to listen to me. I am the ruler of this house." (By the way, if you have to remind your wife constantly that you are the ruler of your house, then you aren't really the ruler.)

If I were holding an open umbrella over my head and someone asked you why I was doing that, you would likely say that it was to protect me from the elements such as rain and wind. When we follow God's plan with regard to marriage and family, we are putting an umbrella of protection around ourselves.

Back in verse 18, the Bible says, *"And be not drunk with wine, wherein is excess; but be filled with the Spirit."* It is absolutely impossible to follow God's plan and pattern in marriage unless we are filled, which in this verse means being controlled by the Holy Spirit. So the first key word is **filled** – not filled with yourself or your problems, but with the Lord.

The second key word is not actually found in these verses, but I believe it speaks to the truth of the passage. That word is **fruitful**. Verse 19 says, *"Speaking to yourselves in psalms and hymns and spiritual songs, singing and making melody in your heart to the Lord."* When you are filled with the Spirit, God gives you a fruitful attitude.

The third key word is **thanksgiving**. Look at verse 20. *"Giving thanks always for all things unto God and the Father in the name of our Lord Jesus Christ."* We are learning to be thankful to Him, not always for our circumstances, but thankful in all things.

Verse 21 contains the fourth key word, which is **submit**. It means "to subdue or put under, to submit oneself to another."

This passage is not speaking primarily about marriage. Once we understand that, we have a grasp of what this chapter in Ephesians is about – the love of Christ for His church, and the church's relationship toward Christ. So while these verses do not speak about marriage first and foremost, marriage is the illustration of the greater issue of Christ's love and the church's submission under Him.

It is a continuation of the opening thought of Ephesians 5, in the first verse: *"Be ye therefore followers of God, as dear children."* It is a picture of the relationship we have with Christ.

Verse 21 tells us to submit, or give ourselves over, *"one to another."* Think of that. I know a lot of men who, when they saw in the table of contents for this book that Ephesians 5 was being covered, would give it to their wives immediately for them to read. But submission is a two-way street. When you are in Christ, there is an equality and a mutual submission between husband and wife.

Let me illustrate this with my own family. In our house, my wife does all of the filing (if I file something, it will never be found). I manage the checkbook, not because I'm better at it, but so that she doesn't have to. She handles our yard work and enjoys it, which is good because I hate yard work.

When it comes to decorating the house, my wife is a former interior decorator so it naturally falls to her. When we go out to eat, I often make the decision regarding where to go because she usually says, "I don't know where I want to go eat."

If you had to sum it up, I probably have more leadership-type roles and she handles more details. But after 40 years of marriage, we are still working at it.

If you ask us what our favorite television programs are, my first instinct might be to say, "I like all of the right ones and she likes all of the wrong ones." But that's just one more example of how we have to give and take with each other. To think that anyone has suddenly arrived in marriage is silly. All of us are still working at it.

Pick out a husband and wife in your church that you think make the ideal married couple. It doesn't matter who it is, but if you are around them long enough, you will see them struggle.

In this passage it is crucial to see the importance of surrender and love. Look at verses 22-24. *"Wives, submit yourselves unto your own husbands, as unto the Lord. ... Therefore as the church is subject unto Christ, so let the wives be to their own husbands in every thing."*

These verses talk about submission, but the Greek word used here is a military term that refers to arranging in order the divisions in a military sense and fashion under the commands of a leader.

Verse 25 says, *"Husbands, love your wives, even as Christ loved the church, and gave himself for it."* This love is expressed by the Greek word *agape*, which is unconditional, God-given love.

The Greek word for *"husband"* in verse 23, along with the phrase *"your own"* that precedes it, would suggest an emphasis on a wife loving only her own husband and not someone else's.

The latter part of that verse directs that this submission is to be *"as unto the Lord."* Many wives who read this might think, "My husband is nothing like the Lord."

Husbands, listen carefully. God ordained that you should be the priest of your family and the spiritual head of your home.

It is interesting that in many churches the wives are the ones who come most often and are willing to do what needs to be done for the Lord's work, and the husbands sit back almost as if they are thinking, "Maybe that will count for me in Heaven also since we are really one." It doesn't work that way.

In the various accounts of Christ's earthly ministry as recorded in the Gospels, the women are always treating Jesus well, almost never speaking against him or hurting him in any way. The ones who were out to get Him were always men.

The concept of submission as an umbrella of protection is not male chauvinism but God's societal order. The family is one of the most basic institutions in society as ordained by God, and He has commanded husbands to love their wives and wives to submit to their husbands.

In Scripture a wife is encouraged to love her husband and follow the example of other Godly women, but a husband is commanded to love his wife. It is a man's job to love his wife. "But you don't know what my wife is like," you might say. Well, you married her. Wives, it is your job to give unto your husband as unto the Lord, no matter you say he's like.

So many men are AWOL on the subject of surrender and love. Look at verse 23. *"For the husband is the head of the wife, even as Christ is the head of the church: and he is the saviour of the body."*

I Cor. 11:3 contains a powerful truth that serves as an example of what we're talking about. *"But I would have you know, that the head of every man is Christ; and the head of the woman is the man; and the head of Christ is God."*

First of all, Paul begins that verse by emphasizing how important it is that we understand what he is writing. That opening phrase is similar to what you might say to your children: "Kids, I want you to get this." He doesn't want us to miss what he is saying.

The final phrase of the verse makes a key theological point. None of us would dispute that Jesus is God. It's what we believe. But this verse refers to a certain order and priesthood. When Christ was on the earth He submitted to His Father's will. The woman-man-Christ-God example perfectly illustrates God's intended order.

Everything has a head, or a leader. In the evil empire of this world it is Satan. In the righteous empire of the world it is Christ. God's order always includes human relationships

Think back to the Garden of Eden. The first man, Adam, was made from the dust of the ground. The first woman, Eve, was taken from his side. I Tim. 2:13-14 makes an interesting observation about their relationship. *"For Adam was first formed, then Eve. And Adam was not deceived, but the woman being deceived was in the transgression."*

Eve was given the responsibility of being in a subordinate (not subservient) position to Adam. Satan persuaded Adam and Eve to reverse their roles. When she took the forbidden fruit, Eve took the place of headship.

Satan clearly aimed the temptation at Eve's mind and engaged her in an intellectual discussion about whether she should do something that God had expressly forbidden. She was deceived. Then along came Adam. He was not deceived, but he disobeyed.

God has said that the man is to be the head of the home, but we live in a world today where women are always trying to be like men. Believe me, ladies, you don't want to be like us. God has made each of us the way we are, and that's what we should be.

The Bible says that just as Christ obeyed the Father, the church is to obey Christ and the wife is to obey the husband. Verse 24 says, *"Therefore as the church is subject unto Christ, so let the wives be to their own husbands* [not someone else's husband] *in every thing."*

The purpose of marriage is to exemplify Christ's love for the church. It is impossible to do this apart from the filling of the Holy Spirit of God.

Many wives are unsure about the order of the marriage relationship because their husbands are unsaved. I Pet. 3:1 says, *"Likewise, ye wives, be in subjection to your own husbands; that, if any obey not the word, they also may without the word be won by the conversation of the wives."* I would encourage every wife to pray for her unsaved husband and live a Christ-like life in front of him.

My father was saved at about the same time I was. For more than 30 years my mother prayed for Dad to come to Christ, and one day he did.

Now it needs to be said that no woman should live in an area of physical and sexual abuse. Anyone who is doing something like that with his wife or children should stop immediately. Do not allow a marriage to go on like that.

God has given a beautiful pattern for us to follow. If a man says, "Listen to me! I'm the head of this home!" or shows that kind of attitude, it's not in sync with God's plan. Can you imagine Christ speaking that way to His church? He sacrificed Himself for the church.

That is emphasized in Paul's exhortation to us in verse 25. *"Husbands, love your wives, even as Christ also loved the church, and gave himself for it."* This is a powerful command to husbands to give unconditional love to their wives, without regard for their own rights. As one commentator put it, "Make much of your wife."

Love is the greatest revelation of God. *"But God commendeth his love toward us, in that, while we were yet sinners, Christ died for us."* (Rom. 5:8) There is *phileo* love, which is a feeling, and *eros* love, which is the flesh. Neither is wrong when in the correct context. But this is *agape* love, which is unconditional. It is God's love.

A tremendous passage concerning principles and discipline in marriage is found in I Cor. 7:1-9. *"Now concerning the things whereof ye wrote unto me: It is good for a man not to touch a woman. Nevertheless, to avoid fornication, let every man have his own wife, and let every woman have her own husband. Let the husband render unto the wife due benevolence: and likewise also the wife unto the husband. The wife hath not power of her own body, but the husband: and likewise also the husband hath not power of his own body, but the wife. Defraud ye not one the other, except it be with consent for a time, that ye may give yourselves to fasting and prayer; and come together again, that Satan tempt you not for your incontinency. But I speak this by permission, and not of commandment. For I would that all men were even as I myself. But every man hath his proper gift of God, one after this manner, and another after that. I say therefore to the unmarried and widows, it is good for them if they abide even as I. But if they cannot contain, let them marry: for it is better to marry than to burn."*

What are these verses saying? First of all, if you are not married, hands off. Sexual relationships are only appropriate within marriage.

Verses 2-3 point out that the proper sexual relationships are well and good, but you must respect your partner's desires as much as you do your own. Verses 4-5 show us that these relationships are to be conducted with respect for the partner as a person, and to recognize that the partner is very important. Verses 6-9 emphasize that appropriate sexual relationships are important so that one does not burn with passion.

With this in mind, look at Eph. 5:25. *"Husbands, love your wives, even as Christ also loved the church, and gave himself for it."* You could substitute *"her"* for *"it"* when referring to the church in that passage, which is instructing men to sacrifice themselves for their wives. John 15:13 says, *"Greater love hath no man than this, that a man lay down his life for his friends."*

My wife has had six surgeries. When she has gone through Caesarean births and faced cancer along with a hip replacement, how stupid could I be not to give myself for her? It's not only the Christian thing to do; it's also the human thing to do.

The Muslim world, when it sees the way we treat each other in our marriages, says, "We want nothing to do with that." They have a right to complain about us in that regard.

When I was in Bible college, I had a wonderful and Godly professor named Paul Griffis. He was a great writer, teacher and theologian whom I loved dearly as one of my mentors in life. When I heard that he had resigned all of his positions and essentially ended his career, I went to visit him and his wife, who had Lou Gehrig's disease.

I walked into the bedroom where she lay and he sat beside her. When her nose began to itch, he scratched it. As he fed her some soup for lunch, they laughed together and had a good time.

The love I saw that day was not a love we naturally have for one another. It was closer to the love that Christ has for His church.

You say, "I can't do that." No, you can't. That's why you are always working at it and you always will be.

Notice the expression of what Paul is talking about in verses 26-27. *"That he might sanctify and cleanse it with the washing of water by the word, That he might present it to himself a glorious church, not having spot, or wrinkle, or any such thing; but that it should be holy and without blemish."*

We see here a love that finds us in our sins, regenerates us, transforms us and enables us. When Jesus looks at the church He sees blemishes, faults and failings. What He sees doesn't really amount to much, but Jesus still loves His church.

Christ loves us despite what we are. Remember when He encountered the woman taken in adultery, and He instructed those who are without sin to cast the first stone. Christ sees the church as holy and without blame.

Look again at verse 26. The word *"sanctify"* means to set apart, and the Greek word for *"washing"* is only used one other time in the Bible, in Titus 3:5. It refers to a vessel for washing and is taken from the beautiful picture of the Old Testament priest.

When he approached God, the priest first came to the brazen altar where an animal was sacrificed and its blood shed. This ritual symbolized the radical cleansing of sin which is the basis for our salvation. Sin makes so deep a stain that it can only be washed away in the blood of the Lord Jesus Christ.

Having been to the altar, the priest then proceeded to the tabernacle where God sat, enthroned in holiness, behind the veil. Coming to the laver, which was made of mirrors, he saw that he was only a few steps from the holy place and already defiled by contact with this world. He did not need a new sacrifice at this point, but he needed to be washed with water to remove the defilement. He needed recurrent cleansing.

The blood of Christ secures our salvation. The water of the Word, though, acts like a laver. Like the mirrors of the Old Testament laver, the Word of God reveals to us the defilements we have picked up just by walking through this evil world. The Word of God is also a cleansing agent which removes the defilement. That is why the Psalmist says in Ps. 119:9, *"Wherewithal shall a young man cleanse his way? by taking heed thereto according to thy word."*

The way that we are cleansed is by the Word of God. The Bible is not meant just to read and memorized and thought about, but it needs to become a part of our lives to the extent that it is changing us on a daily basis.

You cannot be a good husband or a good wife unless you go by the orders given in the Bible. There are a lot of good books on the market today that deal with marriage, and plenty of conferences and seminars to attend, but the best thing you can do for your marriage is obey the Word.

Time magazine, in its Jan. 29, 2007 edition, gave six ways to reduce stress in a marriage. The article talked about how to relax, instructing readers to take a vacation, make some friends, exercise regularly, eat plenty of vegetables and fruits, don't stay up late, and do what you love to do. But the first thing the writer said to do was breathe deeply and meditate.

The editors at Time magazine don't realize how right they are. We need time to meditate, but we must meditate on the Word of God.

If you married today, be thankful for your spouse. Don't go to bed angry with each other. Stay up past midnight if you need to, but settle it. Learn to say, "I'm sorry." There is a slight possibility that you could be wrong.

If you are single and thinking about getting married someday, be patient. Ask God to give you the strength to deal with your physical desires properly.

Realize that as you build your relationship, there is always someone who can get in the middle of it. Remember that you have your **own** wife or your **own** husband.

It is easy in our busy lives to spend more time talking with your coworkers than you do with your spouse. You have to schedule time for one another.

Building a marriage is not easily done, and we live in a culture today that is against marriage. There were fewer divorces in 2006 than in 1990 because more unmarried couples are living together. We live in a society where you can almost do whatever you want, provided it is within the boundaries of the law, but isn't God's plan always the best plan?

Back in Eph. 5:18-21 we see what everything we have talked about is based upon. Being filled with the Spirit and submitting to one another in the fear of God – that, my friends, is worship.

I made a phone call recently to a long-time friend of mine from my former church in Pennsylvania, right after his wife passed away. They were married 60 years and had a great relationship.

This man was a military man, second to the commanding general at the army post in his community. He was a leader's leader, but the loss of his wife left him with a broken heart. I wanted to have some prayer with him and encourage him during this difficult time.

Gentlemen, be thankful if your wife is with you today. Ladies, be thankful your husbands. Be thankful for your children. In all things give thanks.

If you are single, be thankful for that. For some it is not God's intention ever to marry. If you are divorced and rearing children alone, or if you are widowed, God placed you in that situation and He will give you the grace you need. Whatever the situation you are in, be thankful for it.

Be much in prayer if you are thinking about marriage. Ask God to let you know when the right person walks through that door, or when to break it off if that is the appropriate course of action.

When I met Bobbi years ago, I knew she was the one (although she didn't seem to know it about me). She told me, "I have several requirements." I was ready to give into whatever she wanted.

"What do you require?" I asked.

"I'm going to marry a preacher," she said.

I was planning to be a preacher. No problem there.

"I want to marry someone who will stay with me the rest of my life."

I was ready for that one also. I may have wanted it worse than she did.

She had a few other stipulations as well. Looking back, I'm thankful she did that. I knew she was the one for me, and I think the Lord finally convinced her that I was the one for her. But that's the only way for a relationship to proceed – in the Lord.

Marriage is a symbol of Christ and His church. It is an earthly truth that serves as an example of a greater truth. With that in mind, we need to live in the Spirit and let God lead us that way, so that we are fulfilled in what He has given to us.

CHAPTER 16

THE TRIANGLE OF MARRIAGE
Ephesians 5:25-33

—♋♋—

Families are going through difficulties today with compatibility, stress, children and many other issues. People are in second and third marriages, bringing existing children into new relationships. There are all kinds of challenges facing married couples today.

Some of you might be wondering, "How do you get away from problems in a marriage?" You don't. Problems are a part of what marriage is all about.

But we need to understand that marriage is a deeply spiritual issue. We saw back in Eph. 5:18 that the key to the kind of marriage God intends for us to have is the filling of the Holy Spirit. As we look at Biblical principles for married life, God is telling us that we cannot do it alone; we need His help. We must be filled with the Holy Spirit.

In verse 32 of Ephesians 5, this is referred to as "a *great mystery*." The word here for "*mystery*" speaks about something that was hidden previously but is now revealed.

The rest of that verse reminds of what we have already discussed, which is how marriage is a picture of the relationship between Jesus Christ and His church, including the church's submission to Christ.

Draw a triangle in your mind. At the top is the Lord Jesus Christ. At one bottom corner is the husband and at the other is the wife. Obviously there is some distance between the husband and wife at the bottom of the triangle. But as they move up the sides of the triangle and get closer to Christ, they also get closer to each other. In other words, the more we fall in love with Christ, the more we are able to fall in love with each other.

There are a lot of human things one can do to keep a marriage working, such as making enough money, maintaining physical attractiveness, saying the right words, staying away from arguments, etc. But we all know that those things don't last very long. There needs to be a relationship built toward Christ, and the more we build toward Christ the greater our relationship can be with each other.

So the key to a successful marriage is the filling of the Holy Spirit and a willingness to yield to God's Word. As we saw in previous verses in Ephesians 5, the filling of the Spirit and the filling of the Word go hand-in-hand and are simultaneous. The more of God's Word that is in our hearts and minds, the more we are able to become what we need to be.

With that in mind, let's look at Eph. 5:28-29 and see what needs to motivate our marriages today, starting with the self-motive. "*So ought men to love their wives as their own bodies. He that loveth his wife loveth himself. For no man ever yet hated his own flesh; but nourisheth and cherisheth it, even as the Lord the church.*"

Marriage is a physical, psychological and spiritual union. When God placed Adam and Eve in the Garden of Eden, according to Gen. 2:23-24, "*And Adam said, This is now bone of my bones, and flesh of my flesh: she shall be called Woman, because she was taken out of Man. Therefore shall a man leave his father and his mother, and shall cleave unto his wife: and they shall be one flesh.*"

We all read that account and agree that it is God's plan and the right plan, but think about how difficult this can be. A baby is born and grows into a child, starts school at age 5 or younger, goes through elementary and high school, then is off to college. After all of this education and all of these life experiences, this young adult starts to wonder how to find someone to marry and then stick together. It's a challenge, and it's not easy.

Bill Cosby spoke recently at a university and said this to the students: "You are not entitled to anything except to go and find work. That is very American and Biblical. Your parents may not say this to you directly, but you should 'go ye, seek ye, and not come back ye.'"

That's the way it works with children. All of a sudden that baby you once held in your arms is grown, and now he or she must look toward building a marriage and having children without really knowing how to go about it. Children grow up quickly. How will they find the people they are supposed to date, much less those that they should marry?

As I said before, if you are single, you should be thankful for that. But every single person, regardless of age, knows the difficulty in finding a dating relationship and a potential marriage partner. It is not easy today.

In many cultures both past and present, when a person wanted to find someone to marry, the parents would decide who to look for. The decision was made by the parents of the young man and the parents of the young lady, and that is how couples come together. In many cases a steward of the family would help make this happen. The parents might instruct the steward to make sure of compatibility and certain characteristics in the prospective mate, and the process would get underway. There are people of various cultures in my church today who practice this.

Not everyone in the United States in the twenty-first century is completely "Westernized." A few years ago our church had a fairly large gypsy ministry, with more than 100 in attendance on a regular basis. The pastor who led that ministry, Walter Stevens, never met his wife until their wedding day, yet they married and are very much in love today.

Many people wonder if the Bible contains specific guidelines for finding and selecting a marriage partner. The only passage that seems to have these principles is found in a story in Genesis 24, in which Abraham sends a servant off to find a bride for Isaac.

Abraham had been told by God that his descendants would be as the sand of the sea or the stars in the sky. Isaac was the son of promise, so obviously the woman chosen to bear Isaac's children would be a very important choice.

How do you find a wife for the son of promise? I believe that there are 10 Biblical principles found in this story that we can apply today.

Look at Gen. 24:1-3. *"And Abraham was old, and well stricken in age: and the LORD had blessed Abraham in all things. And Abraham said unto his eldest servant of his house, that ruled over all that he had, Put, I pray thee, thy hand under my thigh: And I will make thee swear by the LORD, the God of heaven, and the God of the earth, that thou shalt not take a wife unto my son of the daughters of the Canaanites, among whom I dwell: But thou shalt go unto my country, and to my kindred, and take a wife unto my son Isaac."*

The first rule in these verses is to take a mate of the same faith. The second is what I call cultural acceptability.

Our church in south Florida has many different cultures among those who attend. When you marry across cultures, you must be willing to accept your spouse's cultural differences just as he or she must accept yours.

The third rule is to seek compatibility. The repeated use of *"my"* in verse 4 emphasizes Abraham's wish that his servant find a mate who will get along with Isaac and be suited especially for him. "You know what my son Isaac is like," he might have said. "Find him a good match."

Can you imagine being Abraham's steward and having this kind of responsibility? He must have realized the huge burden on his shoulders as he went off in search of someone not only to please Abraham, but also the God of Abraham.

The fourth principle, divine direction, is found in verse 7. *"The LORD God of heaven, which took me from my father's house, and from the land of my kindred, and which spake unto me, and that sware unto me, saying, Unto thy seed will I give this land; he shall send his angel before thee, and thou shalt take a wife unto my son from thence."* Abraham knew that throughout this important search there would be divine direction from God.

I remember when, as a senior in high school, I heard my youth pastor say, "All of you young men should pray that God will lead you to the person He would have you marry some day." Many youth pastors have said that over the years, and I probably heard it other times without paying much attention. But in my final year of high school I was becoming more impressed to take such matters seriously, and this seemed like a good idea. So I began praying, "Lord, who should I marry?"

As time went on, I suggested to God that when the right girl comes along, He should let me know right away. "I don't want to waste a lot of time on this," I prayed. "I want to get this done."

Then I began to think about what she might look like, or what I thought she should look like. One day I saw just that girl – she is my wife today. "That's the one," I thought.

I went up to introduce myself to Bobbi that first time, ready to share with her the wonderful news that she was the Chosen One for me. Much to my surprise, she was not impressed at all with me at that time. But I finally convinced her, and it has become obvious to many over the years that I have the better end of the deal.

If you are divorced today and wondering what God might have in store for you, let me remind you that He loves you more than you will ever know. You might be a single mom or dad rearing children and thinking that no one can love your children more than you do. But God loves those children more than you do.

Fifth, the relationship should be a two-way street. Look at verse 8. "*And if the woman will not be willing to follow thee, then thou shalt be clear from this my oath: only bring not my son thither again.*"

Sometimes you will hear a man say, "I found the one for me, but she's not interested." He keeps after her until he becomes a pain. This also happens when the gender roles are reversed, with the woman chasing the man. If the relationship is of God, at some point both people will show interest in each other.

Verse 14 shows the sixth point, which is the need for a willing spirit. "*And let it come to pass, that the damsel to whom I shall say, Let down thy pitcher, I pray thee, that I may drink; and she shall say, Drink, and I will give thy camels drink also: let the same be she that thou hast appointed for thy servant Isaac; and thereby shall I know that thou hast shewed kindness unto my master.*"

In verses 12-13 the servant asked the Lord for success in his quest, and verse 14 gives the sign that the woman would be the right one. He knew that if he found someone with a willing spirit, he could be successful.

Verse 16 mentions that the woman *"was very fair to look upon."* The seventh requirement is that the people involved be good-looking.

Let me clarify this point. I believe we all can agree that beauty is in the eye of the beholder. You've probably seen a man with a beautiful woman and wondered, "What was she thinking when she paired up with him?" Sometimes it's the other way around.

Verse 16 also says that she was *"a virgin, neither had any man known her."* This is the eighth rule and it is incredibly important. If you are not a virgin, let me urge you to be one from this day forward. Keep yourself pure until you meet the one that God has for you.

The next point is illustrated in verse 25. *"She said moreover unto him, We have both straw and provender enough, and room to lodge in."* She was a servant.

She had previously told the servant which family she was a member of. He knew about this family already because there had been a relationship with Abraham and his family, and he was able to stay for a while with them. She had a servant's spirit, which is always needed in a marriage.

Finally, in verse 31, we see the confirmation. *"And he said, Come in, thou blessed of the LORD; wherefore standest thou without? for I have prepared the house, and room for the camels."*

She had her brother check him out, and he came back with a good report. "This is a great deal for you, Rebekah," he said.

But the family had to make certain that this was what she wanted to do. Look at verse 58. *"And they called Rebekah, and said unto her, Wilt thou go with this man? And she said, I will go."*

Abraham's servant must have been thrilled at this. He probably couldn't wait to go back home and tell Abraham.

After they began the journey back, we see something wonderful in verse 63-67. *"And Isaac went out to meditate in the field at the eventide: and he lifted up his eyes, and saw, and, behold, the camels were coming. And Rebekah lifted up her eyes, and when she saw Isaac, she lighted off the camel. For she had said unto the servant, What man is this that walketh in the field to meet us? And the servant had said, It is my master: therefore she took a vail, and covered herself. And the servant told Isaac all things that he had done. And Isaac brought her into his mother Sarah's tent, and took Rebekah, and she became his wife; and he loved her: and Isaac was comforted after his mother's death."*

Note Rebekah's question to the servant when she saw Isaac. After all of the miles they had traveled, she knew the one she was coming to meet the first time she saw him. As Gen. 24 concludes we see the first story in the Old Testament portraying this kind of love.

Let's look again at the 10 principles outlined in this story: same faith, cultural acceptability, compatibility, divine direction, two-sided, a willing spirit, good looks, purity, a servant's heart, and confirmation.

In a relationship there is always physical and psychological attraction, but there must also be spiritual union. Marriage involves two people becoming one. Gen. 5:2 says, *"Male and female created he them; and blessed them, and called their name Adam, in the day when they were created."* They were both called by the same name because they were one.

Let me challenge every husband reading this to love his wife, and every wife to take care of her husband. Lest we forget the importance of the story of Isaac and Rebekah that we read a few moments ago, we should realize that without it the Jewish nation might never have gotten off the ground.

Marriage is motivated by a self-motive, but also the supreme motive. We see both of these in verses 28-29 of Ephesians 5. *"So ought men to love their wives as their own bodies. He that loveth his wife loveth himself. For no man ever yet hated his own flesh; but nourisheth and cherisheth it, even as the Lord the church."*

The root word for *"nourisheth"* means to take care of one's flesh. It's the same root word used in Eph. 6:4 to refer to fathers bringing up their children.

The word for *"cherisheth"* speaks of a softening by heat, much like a bird would cover here young with her feathers. It's the idea of fostering a tender care and a tender love. It is interesting that the Apostle Paul, in his letters to the Thessalonians, talks about love for the church and a pastor's heart by comparing it to a mother's love for her children.

The Lord loves the church, and He nourishes it and takes care of it. As far as the Lord is concerned, nothing is too good for the church. When I refer to the church, I mean its people. The church is at the center of Christ's thoughts.

There is something special about having a wife and realizing that person is unique to you. One night I was working late and I called my wife to tell her I'd be home around 8 p.m. I was driving up the expressway at about 9 p.m. when my cell phone rang. It was my wife.

"Are you all right?" she asked.

"Yes," I said. "There's just a lot of traffic."

It was nice to have someone call me just to see if I was OK.

Recently we got a positive report from the doctor about my wife's blood levels, which she has been struggling with for some time now. It made me think about how important she is in my life.

When you look at your wife and see her faults and failures and weaknesses, think about how Jesus looks at the church. What does He see in us? Sometimes I wonder why Jesus would ever love us to begin with. There is nothing is us that would make Him love us.

But He does love us, and the Bible says in I Pet. 4:8 that His love covers a multitude of sins. One reason Eph. 5:32 refers to these relationships as *"a great mystery"* is because when you talk about Christ and His church, you are talking about a boundless love.

You might say, "There is no way I can do what I am being asked to do here in my marriage." You are right. No one is humanly capable of doing this. That is why we must be filled with the Holy Spirit. Marriage becomes a noble dream unless we begin to understand what God is saying to us here about the supreme motive of love.

Many of us have seen a couple depicted in a movie or TV show and thought, "Wow! Why isn't my marriage like that?" It's because what you saw is not real. Those are actors and actresses reciting lines written by someone else. Most of the time, when we see some ideal that we would like our marriage to be, that ideal is not real.

Marriage must be worked at. It is something you have to deal with day in and day out. You don't live "happily ever after." That's not how it works. Everyone who has been married for any length of time has had problems. But marriage is just a noble dream unless you start working it out.

In verses 30-32 we find a few principles relating to Christ's boundless love and the triangle of marriage. First we see a man in Christ's body in verse 30. *"For we are members of his body, of his flesh, and of his bones."* That is an incredible thought that speaks about our unity with Him.

Verses 31-32 talk about the man as Christ's bride. *"For this cause shall a man leave his father and mother, and shall be joined unto his wife, and they two shall be one flesh. This is a great mystery: but I speak concerning Christ and the church."*

Marriage is God's idea and God's ideal. It can be a paradise on this earth and an outpost of Heaven in a sin-cursed world when we understand that there must be an unconditional giving and guarantee of love.

You may think that you can never accomplish this in your present situation. In the Old Testament the prophet Hosea had a wife named Gomer who went out and became a prostitute. But God told Hosea to go back to her.

"Wow," you say. "How could he do that?" He did it so that he could become an example of how God loved the nation of Israel. That story was then put in the Old Testament so it could be an example to all of us.

We read a moment ago about how Isaac loved Rebekah. Did they have days that were less than perfect? Of course they did. But their story reminds us of the final thought in Eph. 5:33. *"Nevertheless let every one of you in particular so love his wife even as himself; and the wife see that she reverence her husband."*

If husbands observe this principle and love their wives, most problems will cease. It's hard to resist love. Likewise, every wife is being instructed here to put her husband on the proper pedestal and admire him rather than someone else's husband. That is the kind of relationship God wants us to have as married couples.

Every one of us, if we want to, can find something better in someone else for a while. But that's not God's plan. He wants husbands to love their wives and wives to lift up their husbands.

So often we hear someone say that this is a 50-50 arrangement, and that sounds pretty good. But by whose standards, mine or hers? It would be very easy for one person to say it's 50-50 and the other to respond, "No, I'm giving 60 percent and she's only giving 40."

When you study these passages, you should realize that marriage is not 50-50, but 100-100. God commands husbands and wives in these verses without telling them to expect anything in return.

A wife should not submit to her husband's bullying, but she shouldn't bully him, either. She should build him up and not tear him down. If a wife refuses to reverence her husband, she begins to dominate him and he becomes resentful. The Lord has given the wife a precious and fragile relationship with her husband, and she holds in her hand the power to nurture her relationship with him through love, encouragement, agreement and thankfulness. She also holds the power to tear him down through control, manipulation, criticism, ingratitude and wrong expectations. Prov. 14:1 says, "Every **wise** woman buildeth her house: but the foolish plucketh it down with her hands."

Husbands, love your wives. If you think she is unlovely, think about how Christ must see the church.

Wives, build up your husbands. Don't tell your boss how great he is and never tell your husband.

We must not fall prey to what Satan would love to see, which is the destruction of the family. There are temptations everywhere. When they come our way, we have to understand God's pattern and His plan.

God is not exalting marriage, but He is using it as an illustration of the greater truth – Christ and His love for the church. If your marriage is in disarray, don't put yourself on a huge guilt trip. Start where you are, and do something about it. If your marriage is going well, watch out for the darts of the devil that will certainly come your way.

If you are single and wondering if God has anything for you in the future, remember how His angel led Abraham's servant and know that the same God is in control of your life today. Purpose in your heart to follow where He leads you.

CHAPTER 17

A FATHER'S WORLD
Ephesians 6:1-4

—⟨⟩⟨⟩—

My wife and I spent several years at the beginning of our married life without children, so I especially remember the joy that came when we first had a little one around the house who called me Dad or Daddy. In fact, when I was in a public place and someone else's child called for Daddy, I would look around and start to respond, because that was **my** name. It was quite an honor to be called Daddy.

A young attorney once said, "The greatest gift I ever received came one Christmas when my dad gave me a small box. Inside was a note that said, 'Son, this year I will give you 365 hours, one hour every day after dinner. We'll talk about what you want to talk about, go where you want to go, play what you want to play. It will be your hour.' My dad not only kept his promise, but every year he renewed it. It is the greatest gift I have ever received in my life. I am the result of time."

Educator Bruce Lockerbie wrote these words: "When I was 11 years old, our family drove from Toronto to eastern Ontario, to the region north of the St. Lawrence River where my father had been born. We reached the little village of Spencerville just before midnight. Its residents had long since gone to bed, but Dad needed directions to find the old homestead where we would spend the evening. Reluctantly, he stopped at a darkened house and knocked at the door. After several minutes of waiting the yard light came on and an old man came to the door. I could hear my father apologizing for the inconvenience, but then he identified himself as the son of Pearson Lockerbie. My grandfather had been dead for many years, but when the man at the door heard that name he said, 'Come on in. I remember your father well.' That is perhaps the greatest legacy a man can leave his son – a legacy of being well-known with such character."

We hear a lot about women today. When you prepare a message on Mother's Day you have plenty of material at your disposal. You have to dig a little bit when looking for material about fathers.

But we need men of God today who are, first and foremost, men of God in their homes. As we read and study Eph. 6:1-4, let's think about a father's world.

"Children, obey your parents in the Lord: for this is right. Honour thy father and mother; which is the first commandment with promise; That it may be well with thee, and thou mayest live long on the earth.." And, ye fathers, provoke not your children to wrath: but bring them up in the nurture and admonition of the Lord.

In a father's world, there is a child's task. Verses 1-3 speak about a child's responsibility to God, and the parents are guardians. In other words, a child is to be taught something about authority and responsibility to God by the parents.

When a child defies parental authority or is supported by the parents to defy God-given authority, the child learns to defy divine authority. There is authority with parents, school, church, government – all kinds of God-given authority, and we need each other to raise our children. When we are harsh toward church or school or whatever clubs or organizations our children may be involved in, we are teaching our children that they can rebel against God-given authority.

So many times we have heard about the parent who takes the side of the child against the teacher at school. Years later, when the child rebels against the parent, that parent has nowhere to go because the child has been taught to practice rebellion. This passage teaches that a child has a responsibility to those in authority.

172

Something very interesting is written about our Lord in Luke 2. Jesus had gone to the temple and answered questions, and His parents had lost track of Him when they started home. We see a familiar passage in verses 48-49: *"And when they saw him, they were amazed: and his mother said unto him, Son, why hast thou thus dealt with us? behold, thy father and I have sought thee sorrowing. And he said unto them, How is it that ye sought me? wist ye not that I must be about my Father's business?"*

It seems almost that He is rebellious toward Mary and Joseph, but this is not the case. Look at verses 50-51. *"And they understood not the saying which he spake unto them. And he went down with them, and came to Nazareth, and was subject unto them: but his mother kept all these sayings in her heart."*

So the Son of God returned with His earthly parents and remained under their authority in Nazareth. We need to train our children to be responsible to God-given authority.

We also see a principle of respect for God through honoring our father and mother. The word *"honor"* in verse 2 means to hold up as precious and valuable. We should speak well of our parents. When a child honors his parents, he is essentially honoring the Lord.

We talk often about the Ten Commandments, and it is frequently said that the first four commandments are toward God and the last six are toward each other. In fact, the first five are really directed toward God.

Look at Exodus 20, starting with verses 1-2. *"And God spake all these words, saying, I am the LORD thy God, which have brought thee out of the land of Egypt, out of the house of bondage."* Throughout this passage there is a continual emphasis on *"the LORD thy God."*

This continues in verses 3-5. *"Thou shalt have no other gods before me. Thou shalt not make unto thee any graven image, or any likeness of any thing that is in heaven above, or that is in the earth beneath, or that is in the water under the earth. Thou shalt not bow down thyself to them, nor serve them: for I the LORD thy God am a jealous God, visiting the iniquity of the fathers upon the children unto the third and fourth generation of them that hate me."*

There is more of this in verse 7. *"Thou shalt not take the name of the LORD thy God in vain; for the LORD will not hold him guilt-*

less that taketh his name in vain." Once again, the emphasis is on the Lord.

Verses 8-11: *"Remember the sabbath day, to keep it holy. Six days shalt thou labour, and do all thy work: But the seventh day is the sabbath of the LORD thy God: in it thou shalt not do any work, thou, nor thy son, nor thy daughter, thy manservant, nor thy maidservant, nor thy cattle, nor thy stranger that is within thy gates: For in six days the LORD made heaven and earth, the sea, and all that in them is, and rested the seventh day: wherefore the LORD blessed the sabbath day, and hallowed it."* We now know that the Sabbath has been fulfilled on the first day of the week due to the Resurrection, but the emphasis is again on *"the LORD thy God."*

These commandments obviously refer to our relationship with God, but look at verse 12. *"Honour thy father and thy mother: that thy days may be long upon the land which the LORD thy God giveth thee."* There is more emphasis on the Lord, so actually the first five commandments are toward God. When you honor your father and mother, you are honoring God.

Some of you may have been raised in an environment you did not know your father or your mother. Perhaps you grew up with another guardian. No matter who had the task of your upbringing, you should give honor to whom it is due.

My wife and I decided a long time ago that we wanted to be there for our parents whenever we could. My dad died rather quickly of a heart attack but my mom lived well into her nineties and was in good health until about age 90. She started to deteriorate the last two or three years of her life. My two sisters lived away from her, and my brother lived far away, although they came and helped out whenever they had the opportunity. So a great deal of the responsibility for her care fell upon me and my wife, and my wife especially spent a lot of time caring for her in those final few years while I was working. We added an apartment for my mother onto our house and did a number of other special modifications.

When my wife and I look back on that time, we consider ourselves blessed to have been able to care for my mother. I believe it is Scriptural for all of us to look after our parents as they get older.

A cover story in the June 18, 2007 edition of Newsweek was titled, "Confronting Alzheimer's: Millions of boomers are caring for parents afflicted with a disease that steals minds and memories. What life is like when your mother doesn't know you, or her own name."

Here is a brief excerpt from that story:

A man is sitting next to her. She knows his name is Frank, but that is all she knows. She doesn't remember that when they met, she was head cheerleader and he was considered the best-looking guy in town.

She doesn't remember that they've been married nearly 63 years and have raised two daughters, Michel Webb, 55, and Melinda Proza, 46. She doesn't know that her daughters and Frank, 85, try to watch her constantly because they're terrified she will wander off.

She doesn't even know her own name. It is Helen Erskine. She is 81 years old and she has Alzheimer's disease — a devastating diagnosis.

"Only people who have this in their family could possibly understand what we're going through," says Webb, a Dallas banker.

With other diseases, she says, "there's usually a progression, a treatment, and you're hopeful for a positive end. With Alzheimer's, there is no positive end."

The final paragraph of the story, which refers to another family facing this same situation, is especially noteworthy. Look at what this woman's daughter says about her mother:

"When we were kids, they cared for us," she says. "Now it's our turn." That kind of love is not just a memory.

When God says in His Word that we should honor our parents, that is what He is talking about. I realize that sometimes people live far away from their parents and it is often necessary to utilize an assisted-living facility or nursing home, but no matter how old we get, we should always remember the importance of honoring Mom and Dad.

This passage in Ephesians 6 also contains a promise. It is in verse 3: *"That it may be well with thee, and thou mayest live long on the earth."*

What does this mean? Sometimes we see children taken to Heaven as infants or before five years of age, or we know of teens who die in auto accidents. So what exactly is this verse talking about?

The Bible says in Heb. 9:27, *"And as it is appointed unto men once to die, but after this the judgment."* In other words, death carries with it an appointed time. There is a place and a time that we will all die. (I like to joke with people that if I knew the place I was going to die, I would never go there.)

God may want some of us to live only five years, or 15. For others, His plan might be to live 80 or 90 years. We do not know how long He has planned for each of us. But if you honor your father and mother you can live out all of the time God has for you.

Jerry Falwell put it well when he said, "If you are a man or woman of God, you are indestructible until God is ready to call you home." That is especially true when we take care to honor our parents.

In a father's world, there is a trust factor. Look at verse 4. *"And, ye fathers, provoke not your children to wrath: but bring them up in the nurture and admonition of the Lord."*

When this verse talks about bringing up children, it is the same as when Eph. 5:29 refers to a husband nourishing his wife.

In Col. 3:21 the Bible says, *"Fathers, provoke not your children to anger, lest they be discouraged."* It is an interesting thought that children can become discouraged if we provoke them. But we see in two separate passages the importance of not provoking your children.

The word *"provoke"* means to make bitter or stimulate to bitterness.

I spoke recently at a church in Delaware for a good friend and flew back to Miami from Philadelphia late on a Sunday night. The airport was packed, and I sat down next to a man who was talking on his cell phone. I believe everyone at the gate could hear his conversation.

From what I could tell from his loud voice and the things he was saying, he appeared to be talking to one of his children. He was berating him, just tearing into him. Suddenly, in the middle of the conversation, he said, "Wait a minute. I've got the old man on the other line." He switched lines and chewed out his father a little for interrupting him, then he eventually went back to the original conversation.

"Wow," I thought. "What a family that must be."

Heb. 3:8 says, "Harden not your hearts, as in the provocation, in the day of temptation in the wilderness." The passage is talking about the time the children of Israel spent in the wilderness. That *"provocation"* is from the same root word as we read earlier in Eph. 4:30 that refers to grieving the Holy Spirit. When all of these passages are looked at together, we see the seriousness of provoking our children and causing them to be bitter.

Children are not mindless objects to be bullied and bossed around. They have thoughts and feelings. But if you have children, you know how difficult it is sometimes to deal with them. Many of us have strong-willed children, and some have children who are shy, quiet and compliant. But God does not address these differences in this passage. He simply commands us not to provoke our children.

Children need good role models, and we should be the best ones. Consider this poem:

> There are little eyes upon you, and they're watching night and
> day.
> There are little ears that quickly take in everything you say.
> There are little hands that are eager to do everything you do,
> And a little boy who's dreaming of the day he'll be like you.
> You're the little fellow's idol, you're the wisest of the wise.
> His little mind about you has no suspicions that ever arise.
> He believes in you devoutly and holds all you say and do;
> He will say and do in your way when he's grown up, just like
> you.
> He's a wide-eyed little fellow who believes you're always doing
> right
> And his ears are always open, watching day and night.

You are setting an example every day in all you do
For the little boy who's waiting to grow up to be just like you.

My father died years ago. He was a good father, but he's gone. What is the most important thing he could have given me?

He had a business. He came to me one day and said, "If you want the business, you can have it." I had been called into the ministry so I didn't take over the business. But was that the best thing he could have given me?

He sent me to college and encouraged me to get a good education and make a lot of money. But was that the best thing he could have given me?

I believe with all my heart that the best thing a son or a daughter could receive from a father is a role model that loves the Lord and always points his children to Him. It is likely that our children will not have us with them their entire lives. When that child in the poem we just read grows up to be an adult, he may not look to his father like he did when he was a little boy. You children need you to point them to the Lord, and not just for salvation.

When my dad received Christ, our family went to church every time the doors were open. We went Sunday morning, Sunday night and Wednesday night. If there was an eight-day revival, we went to every one of the meetings.

I would often think as a child that I didn't want to go, and I sometimes tried to make myself seem sick so I could stay home. Nothing worked with him. He placed me in an atmosphere that, to this day, I am thankful for.

That is a father's responsibility. Some men might say, "Well, my wife's more spiritual than I am." If that's true, shame on you.

In today society's there are so many women working outside the home and many of them earn more money than their husbands. In a lot of cases the men take a back seat and forget that they are to be the spiritual leaders of their homes. You can't let the church or the school do what should be done in the home, and whenever there are two parents in the home the spiritual leader should be the husband.

These verses in Ephesians 6 point out a method, but there is also a motive. Notice how the latter part of verse 4 talks about bringing up, or nurturing, children. In Old Testament days an Israelite child would ask his father about the Passover and the father would explain this important tradition. Special signs and verses would be placed on the door posts during this time. The people were training and teaching the children this way – nurturing them.

I used to pitch softball, and my father taught me. We lived in upstate New York and had an old banged-up garage in the back yard. He would stand a few yards in front of that garage with his glove and tell me, "Throw the ball into the glove. If you throw it to me, I'll catch it. If you throw it outside, you'll have to go get it."

I can't tell you how upset I would get about that. For a long time, I would have to go get the ball and come back after each throw. But after a while I started hitting the glove every time. Then when I pitched in a game, I would say to myself, "Hit the glove." There were plenty of times the batter hit it a long way in the opposite direction, but I hit the glove. That was the result of the way my father taught me and disciplined me.

A teenage girl once said, "My parents never cared enough about me to discipline me." Another teen said, "My father used a cannon to kill a mosquito when he disciplined me." Neither approach is the right one. Prov. 13:24 says, *"He that spareth the rod hateth his son."*

Eph. 6:4 refers to nurturing as well as admonition. In I Corinthians 10 the Apostle Paul begins by saying, *"I would not that ye should be ignorant."* He then writes some important things about the children of Israel, concluding with verses 10-11: *"Neither murmur ye, as some of them also murmured, and were destroyed of the destroyer. Now all these things happened unto them for examples: and they are written for our admonition, upon whom the ends of the world are come."*

In other words, this passage is for our instruction and encouragement. Many of the stories in the Old Testament were written so that we can know what the people learned. The synonym of the Greek word used here is *paideia*, which means "training by an act." The word here means "training by the word." When training and admonishing our children, we need to say it and act it.

In I Sam. 2:25, Eli bemoaned the fact that the people *"hearkened not unto the voice of their father."* All fathers have problems when rearing their children, and they often wonder what their children are thinking or why they are acting the way they are. Sometimes your children embarrass you or say things that you wish had never been said. They might spend time with the wrong crowd as teenagers or go off to college and never call home. There comes a time in the rearing of a child when you realize the importance and absolute power of prayer.

Jerry Williamson, a pastor friend of mine in south Florida, told me once that he was worried about a grown child. He went to a lady with several adult children and asked her, "How do you deal with a son who is grown?"

She gave some great advice. "There comes a day," she said, "when it's 'hands off' and 'prayer on.'"

I realize that we do not become totally "hands off," but at this point we need to really put prayer on our children.

If there is one thing a child needs from a father, it is the knowledge that he or she can trust Dad. My father knew things about me that no one else knew, and I didn't want anyone else to know about them. He went to his grave knowing those things about me.

Chuck Swindoll once said:

I remember stealing six softballs when I worked as a stock boy in my high school years. I tried to find a place to hide them when I went home. I didn't know what I would do with six softballs, and to this day it baffles me why I stole them, but I hid them in the back of my drawer and my mother found them. [Isn't it amazing how mothers always find things?]

My father presented them to me and told me we were going to make a trip back to the store where I would confess. I was dying just thinking about standing in front of my employer.

When I told the store owner what I had done, my dad was waiting in the car. The store owner told me, "You're fired."

I stumbled back to the car and sat down, as low as I could ever remember being. On the way home my dad began rebuilding my emotions. I had done wrong and learned an incredible lesson.

Without overdoing it, he drilled into me that when you steal, you get fired and you lose something that cannot be bought at any price – your self-respect.

But there was something about the ornament of grace that came around the neck of my father, and as we walked into the house he put his arm around me and helped me understand.

You see, this teenage boy was most concerned that his dad not tell any of his friends about this. As far as I know, he took this story to his grave and never told anyone.

We are so shocked at times when our children do wrong. "Do you mean to tell me that my child did **that**?" You tell off the teacher, the youth pastor, the pastor, or the store owner for even suggesting that your little angel could have done that.

But when you build trust in your family's life, there is a love and compassion you have that compels you to protect your children but also tell them, "You've got to live the right way."

Dad, you need to be the leader in your home. "But my wife's smarter than I am," you say. Most wives are smarter than their husbands in a lot of ways. But God commanded husbands and fathers to be the leaders in their homes.

Don't be afraid to carry your Bible with you or know what it says. Don't be afraid, when women come along and try to tempt you away from your family, to say, "I can't. I have a home, a wife, and children."

Be the one in your home to stand up and say, "We're going to be a family that follows the Lord and the Bible."

My dad was about 50 years old when he got saved, and he didn't know anything about the Bible. My mom knew a lot, because she was saved as a child. Dad would say, "We're going to read the Bible," and he didn't even know where to start. But he knew he was supposed to do it.

We need a nation of godly men today. Purpose in your heart that you will be one of them.

CHAPTER 18

WHO'S THE BOSS?
Ephesians 6:5-9

—⟨⟩⟨⟩—

R ecently I was reading about an elderly widow who was restricted in her activities but eager to serve Christ. She soon realized that she could be a blessing to people by playing the piano, so she put this small ad in the Oakland Tribune: "Pianist will play hymns by phone daily for the sick and despondent. The service is free."

The notice included a phone number, and whenever someone called she would ask what hymn that person wanted to hear.

Within a few months, the response was phenomenal. People were calling all day, and many wanted her help with ministry. She was an encourager. A God-glorifying ministry was accomplished by an unlikely person in an unlikely place and in an unlikely way.

Here is a question for you to consider: What about ministry in slavery? Can you do ministry as a slave? Maybe it depends upon knowing who your boss is.

Slavery is an issue that has to be dealt with in context, and before you can understand how a passage of Scripture applies to your life we need to know what the Bible teaches in its context. A young Christian can read some of these passages and wonder, "Why doesn't Jesus or Paul come down hard against slavery? Why don't they call for its abolition?"

It seems that it would be a lot easier for us in our Christian lives if, particularly on hot-button issues like slavery and abortion, we had specific verses in the Bible that read, "This is wrong. Don't do it." That's not the case, however. But we can gain some context and clear up some of the contradictions and misconceptions regarding these issues, and that will allow us to move forward in our Christian walk.

Look at Eph. 6:5. *"Servants, be obedient to them that are your masters according to the flesh, with fear and trembling, in singleness of your heart, as unto Christ."* That first word, *"servants,"* is also translated as "slaves" or "bondservants."

A slave was a person bound to another for labor. He was owned as property by another. Slavery was widespread in the ancient Near East, although the economy was not dependent upon it. In fact, it is estimated that during the height of the Roman Empire, between one-third and one-half of the total Roman population was made up of slaves.

But this was already so common that people were used to it. The history of slavery dates back many centuries before the New Testament. You may recall that Hagar, who gave birth to Abraham's son Ishmael, was a slave. Joseph was sold into slavery by his own brothers for 20 shekels, and from about 3,000 B.C. until a few hundred years ago captives of war were the primary source of slaves.

Slavery was highly regulated in Jewish culture. A Jew could not keep another Jew in perpetual slavery. Jewish slaves were freed every six years, and during the Year of Jubilee they were freed no matter how long they had been slaves.

In Samaritan society slaves had legal rights. They could borrow money and even engage in certain business practices. Slaves received the best treatment in Greek and Roman society, where they were so great in number. They often became hired servants and good friends of their masters, and they were often able to buy their own freedom. In some ways it was better to be a slave 2,000 years ago than it would be to live in the United States in the 1900s or in some Third World countries today.

The New Testament attitude indicates that a slave at that time was more like a hired servant in an employer-employee relationship. It appears that, when these verses in Ephesians were written, the practice of slavery was beginning to slowly decline.

It is true that there was no strong opposition to slavery from Jesus or His apostles. Instead, slaves and servants were admonished to serve their masters faithfully, and masters were told to treat their slaves humanely, as we see in Eph. 6:8-9 as well as Colossians 4, I Timothy 2 and Philemon 16. In fact, the prophet Amos condemned two neighboring nations to Israel for their practice of keeping entire populations in bondage. There is a lot of negativity toward slavery in the Bible, and although Paul never preached against slavery, he worked for the freedom of the slave Onesimus as recorded in the book of Philemon.

It is consistent with New Testament theology that there is no explicit condemnation of slavery, but it implies that in Christ we are free anyway. Galatians 4 tells us that there is neither Jew nor Gentile, male or female, slave or free at the foot of the cross. That is good news. Acts 17:26 says, *"And hath made of one blood all nations of men for to dwell on all the face of the earth, and hath determined the times before appointed, and the bounds of their habitation."* We are all equal at the cross.

You might be wondering, "That all sounds good, but what about these professing Christians who abused this institution?" You probably know this already, but some of our Founding Fathers owned slaves. They traded them, bought and sold them. But I believe our Christian heritage opposes slavery.

God has always ordained the transforming of cultures, societies and nations not through policies and politics, but through the gospel of the Lord Jesus Christ. He transforms people from the inside out. Christ said to Caesar in Matt. 22:21, "Render therefore unto Caesar the things which are Caesar's; and unto God the things that are God's." Jesus was apolitical when it came to public policy and issues.

The Sermon on the Mount was not a sermon on slavery or political issues and themes that were going on at that time in Rome. It was about His Kingdom and the Kingdom to come. That's how the Lord operates, and it was the same with Paul. Ministry superseded slavery, and we can grasp this when we understand who our boss is.

In Eph. 6:5-9, the Apostle Paul writes, *"Servants, be obedient to them that are your masters according to the flesh, with fear and trembling, in singleness of your heart, as unto Christ; Not with eyeservice, as menpleasers; but as the servants of Christ, doing the will of God from the heart; With good will doing service, as to the Lord, and not to men: Knowing that whatsoever good thing any man doeth, the same shall he receive of the Lord, whether he be bond or free. And, ye masters, do the same things unto them, forbearing threatening: knowing that your Master also is in heaven; neither is there respect of persons with him."*

There were some great Christians in centuries past who opposed slavery on Biblical principles. The film "Amazing Grace" is the story of a great man named William Wilberforce. He was a politician in England and became a Christian philanthropist, but he devoted his life to striving for the abolition of the African slave trade. He was one of the leaders of the abolitionist movement. A devout Anglican, he used Christian morals to argue against slavery. There is a historically black college in Ohio named after him – Wilberforce University.

In 1797, ten years after his struggle began, Wilberforce wrote, "The grand object of my parliamentary existence is the abolition of the slave trade. If it please God to honor me so far, may I be the instrument of stopping such a course of wickedness and cruelty as never before has graced a Christian country." He knew that Christianity and slavery, at the heart, were incompatible.

The victory finally came for him in 1807 when the royal assent was declared. The battle wasn't over completely; he fought on until his death in 1833. Not only was it a controversial battle, but the decisive vote of victory that abolished slavery completely was taken three days before he died.

Everyone remembers Dr. Martin Luther King Jr. as a civil rights leader. He was the pastor of the Ebenezer Baptist Church in Atlanta and founder of the Southern Christian Leadership Conference. He wrote these words in April of 1963: "As the Apostle Paul carried the gospel of Christ, so am I compelled to carry the gospel, and one day the South will know that when these disinherited children of God sat down at lunch counters, they were standing up for what is best in the American dream and for the most sacred of values in our Judeo-Christian heritage."

So slavery is not compatible with Christianity. But in the passage we're looking at in Ephesians, the Lord has bigger issues on His mind. Ministry supersedes slavery.

There are two main ideas I want to convey from these verses. The first is that you have ministry to your earthly boss. The word *"obedient"* in verse 5 comes from the same root word as another key word we've seen throughout the book of Ephesians – submission. It's from the Greek word *hupitaso*, a military term that refers to coming under authority, getting in line or in order of rank. It doesn't mean the master or employer is superior to the bondservant or employee, but God has ordained institutions in the workplace so that there must be leaders as well as followers.

This is consistent with the rest of the book of Ephesians. Your true ID tells you that, as a new man or woman in Jesus Christ, you walk in Christ by being filled with the Holy Spirit and that always leads to submission. As we have seen in the marriage relationship and the parent-child relationship, the employer-employee relationship requires submission to be successful.

In a practical sense, this means that you must obey the commands of your employer – even the ones you don't like – just as we are to submit to the governing authorities in our lives, as Paul writes in Romans 13.

I Peter 2:18-19 says, *"Servants, be subject to your masters with all fear; not only to the good and gentle, but also to the froward. For this is thankworthy, if a man for conscience toward God endure grief, suffering wrongfully."* These words were first directed at persecuted Christians who were understandably hesitant to heed the admonition to remain submissive to their government.

The Christian life is not supposed to be easy. There is no prosperity gospel. Despite what you may hear in some circles, God does not necessarily want you to be healthy and wealthy. To the contrary, Paul told Timothy that those who wish to live a godly life can expect to suffer. Some of that suffering will likely be in the workplace, and we are still to submit.

Not only is submission to your earthly boss expected, but there is to be submission with a godly attitude. We all know that people can obey commands without the right attitude. You can probably think of plenty of times when you've given your children a command and it was met with grumbling, even as they carried out their assignments. But it's not much of a ministry if a Christian employee, when given instructions by a secular boss, grumbles about it even while doing it.

Think for a moment about the phrase *"with eyeservice, as menpleasers"* in verse 6. We've all been guilty of it at one time or another. You're relaxing a little bit at work, goofing off or making a few personal phone calls, when the boss comes around the corner. Suddenly you're shuffling papers on your desks in a mad attempt to look busy. You want to make it look like you're doing your job and keep the boss happy, even when you're not really working. After the boss leaves, you go right back to goofing off. That is what this passage is referring to. Are you working for the Lord, doing ministry for your earthly boss, when you behave like that? I don't think so.

Another key phrase here is "with *fear and trembling*" in verse 5. That doesn't mean that you cower in front of your employers, but you have reverence and respect for their authority. They are due honor and respect from their Christian employees. Working *"in singleness of your heart"* means doing the job with diligence – saying to yourself, "This is what I'm supposed to do, and I'm going to do it."

This concept is repeated in Col. 3:22-23, the latter verse of which we all know very well. *"Servants, obey in all things your masters according to the flesh; not with eyeservice, as menpleasers; but in singleness of heart, fearing God; And whatsoever ye do, do it heartily, as to the Lord, and not unto men."*

God is our primary boss. He is our ultimate commander-in-chief who gives us our marching orders. Remembering this can help us deal with these passages in their proper context and accept instructions that may seem difficult at times to carry out. Put simply, we need to remember who is the boss.

Many of you may be in situations at work where you have a very bad earthly boss. He or she may not be a Christian and might be difficult or abusive. What do you do? For some, the response is, "I'm out of here. This person is driving me nuts."

Paul had something interesting to say about that in I Cor. 7:17. *"But as God hath distributed to every man, as the Lord hath called every one, so let him walk. And so ordain I in all churches."* God is not caught by surprise in whatever is happening to you.

We see this thought in greater detail in I Cor. 7:20-24. *"Let every man abide in the same calling wherein he was called. Art thou called being a servant? care not for it: but if thou mayest be made free, use it rather. For he that is called in the Lord, being a servant, is the Lord's freeman: likewise also he that is called, being free, is Christ's servant. Ye are bought with a price; be not ye the servants of men. Brethren, let every man, wherein he is called, therein abide with God."*

Ministry is the priority, not comfort in the workplace. Of course, I'm not talking about true physical slavery or abuse, but if you are in a difficult situation at work, should you leave it? Or are you called by God to minister to fellow employees (and your employer) in that situation?

Paul is encouraging us here to stay where we are and not be in a rush to leave our situation. This also applies to being single or married. He writes that being single is a gift and not to be in a hurry to give it up, and a person who is married should not be rushing to give up his or her spouse due to a difficult situation.

"Stay where you are," God is saying. "I've got something good for you."

Another thing to keep in mind is that, in your workplace, you may be the only one bringing salt and light into the lives of your coworkers. You might be the only Christian in your department or even in your entire company.

I know someone who is working for a boss who can be evil at times. My friend has been mocked because of his faith while at his job, but he is leading people to Christ there at the same time. Fellow employees who are pagans and live in all kinds of wickedness are coming to him now and asking him questions about the Bible and why he lives the way he does. He is honoring his true boss, his King, by giving out salt and light in his workplace. Even though has been tempted to leave, he stays committed because he sees his ministry there.

God knows your situation. He is sovereign and He is never caught by surprise. He knows who your boss is and how difficult your work may be.

Prov. 16:9 says, "*A man's heart deviseth his way: but the LORD directeth his steps.*" We have all of these plans for how long we go to school, what we will study, and where and how long we will work after that. But God actually is calling the shots.

Prov. 16:33 says, "The lot is cast into the lap; but the whole disposing thereof is of the LORD." God makes every decision. One of the most incredible things to me about God is how He takes every circumstance and works them together according to His perfect plan. **He is working right now in the lives of billions of people at one time.** If you think about that long enough, your head would probably hurt. That is a mind-blowing attribute of God.

You have ministry to your earthly boss, but you also have ministry to your heavenly Boss. Look again at Eph. 6:8. "*Knowing that whatsoever good thing any man doeth, the same shall he receive of the Lord, whether he be bond or free.*" God is going to give you what He wants to give you. This verse points out that we will be provided for when we do as He has commanded and be the employees we should be in the workplace.

The principle is paralleled again in Col. 3:24-25. "*Knowing that of the Lord ye shall receive the reward of the inheritance: for ye serve the Lord Christ. But he that doeth wrong shall receive for the wrong which he hath done: and there is no respect of persons.*" It is the common-sense principle of sowing and reaping.

Rewards as expressed in the Bible are spiritual and they are heavenly. Only on occasion does the Bible talk about material rewards. Sometimes you will receive a material reward for a job well done and sometimes you will not. The 12 disciples of Jesus Christ who turned the world upside-down some 2,000 years ago were not wealthy men in a material sense.

There is no crime in being rich. The important thing is what you do with what you have. Consider the words of Solomon, the richest man who ever lived, in the latter portion of Prov. 11:18. "To him that soweth righteousness shall be a sure reward."

The book of Ruth has a wonderful illustration of this. Boaz, in encouraging his wife-to-be for her sacrifice in coming from Moab with her mother-in-law back to Bethlehem, told her in Ruth 2:12, *"The LORD recompense thy work, and a full reward be given thee of the LORD God of Israel, under whose wings thou art come to trust."* She received a just reward.

Christ tells us to have a "beautitude attitude" about this. In Matt. 5:12, during the Sermon on the Mount, He said, *"Rejoice, and be exceeding glad: for great is your reward in heaven: for so persecuted they the prophets which were before you."* The first part of that verse sounds great, but we don't like that second part so much.

Ps. 19:7-11 tells us about enjoyable it is to partake of the Word of God. *"The law of the LORD is perfect, converting the soul: the testimony of the LORD is sure, making wise the simple. The statutes of the LORD are right, rejoicing the heart: the commandment of the LORD is pure, enlightening the eyes. The fear of the LORD is clean, enduring for ever: the judgments of the LORD are true and righteous altogether. More to be desired are they than gold, yea, than much fine gold: sweeter also than honey and the honeycomb. Moreover by them is thy servant warned: and in keeping of them there is great reward."*

When you obey God, you are rewarded. He doesn't say how, but it will happen, even if you have a rotten boss in the workplace.

Ministry to an earthly boss also means that those in authority are commanded to rule with a godly attitude. If you are a CEO or a manager, having employees working under you and answering to you, or if you are an entrepreneur working for yourself, Eph. 6:9 is for you. *"And, ye masters, do the same things unto them, forbearing threatening: knowing that your Master also is in heaven; neither is there respect of persons with him."*

C.S. Lewis is quoted as saying, "Aristotle said some people are only fit to be slaves. I do not contradict him, but I reject slavery because I see no men fit to be masters."

Abuse does not have to be physical. It can be verbal, as in continued berating of employees. It can be a command to work over time during a holiday or some other important time to the employee personally. It can be a "my way or the highway" attitude from an employer.

To be the right kind of master and also minister to our heavenly Boss means that we must be just and right. In this passage, masters and servants have the same accountability to God. Jesus has taught us that you cannot be an effective leader until you have been an effective servant. He said so in Matt. 20:26-27. "But it shall not be so among you: but whosoever will be great among you, let him be your minister; And whosoever will be chief among you, let him be your servant."

Christ put actions to those words in John 13 when He performed the foot-washing for His disciples – including Judas, whom He already knew would later betray Him. The King of Kings and Lord of Lords performed the most menial task that a slave in first-century Palestine could perform, on His hands and knees washing dirty feet. By doing this for the disciples, He showed us a picture of what He has done for us.

This model of servanthood goes back to the book of Genesis. Joseph was a slave and a servant before becoming the most powerful man in Egypt (and perhaps the known world) during his time. Moses, Joshua, David and Jeremiah are other Old Testament examples of this rise from servant status to great leadership. It's why Vance Havner said, "A leader is a person with a magnet in his heart and a compass in his head."

All earthly bosses should remember that their employees are due justice and grace. This was illustrated in the parable of the talents. Matt. 25:21 says, "*His lord said unto him, Well done, thou good and faithful servant: thou hast been faithful over a few things, I will make thee ruler over many things: enter thou into the joy of thy lord.*"

If you want to do more for the Kingdom, do well with what you have. Be responsible and compassionate, just and gracious, as your Lord is, especially those of you who are earthly masters serving a heavenly Boss.

A final example of how an employer-employee relationship should be is found in Ruth 2:4. "*And, behold, Boaz came from Bethlehem, and said unto the reapers, The LORD be with you. And they answered him, The LORD bless thee."* Boaz had a heart for his employees, and he treated them well. In return, his workers loved and respected him.

Whether you are a servant or a master, an employee or an employer, you should be faithful to your calling. Wherever you are, whatever you are doing, consider staying put. You are a minister in the workplace, no matter what your position may be. You have a ministry to your earthly boss, but more importantly, you also have a ministry to your heavenly Boss.

Consider these points from David Ausberger's book "Enough is Enough":

People are illogical, unreasonable and self-centered. Love them anyway.

If you do good, people will accuse you of selfish ulterior motives. Do good anyway.

If you're successful, you'll win false friends and true enemies. Succeed anyway.

The good you do today will be forgotten tomorrow. Do good anyway.

Honesty and frankness make you vulnerable. Be honest and frank anyway.

The biggest men with the biggest ideas can be shot down by the smallest men with the smallest minds. Think big anyway.

People favor underdogs but only follow top dogs. Fight for a few underdogs anyway.

What you spend years building may be destroyed overnight. Build anyway.

People really need help but may attack you if you help them. Help them anyway.

Give the world the best you have and you're going to get kicked in the teeth. Give the world your best anyway.

When you really get to know who your Boss is and start working for Him, it will transform your life in the workplace. You will see it as a ministry. Then, when you receive your just rewards, He will look at you and say, "Well done, good and faithful servant." That's what you want to hear.

CHAPTER 19

THE FULL ARMOR
Ephesians 6:10-18

_____ යි ෙ _____

This chapter is designed to prepare you for war.

War against terrorism is in the headlines every day. At this writing, that conflict has been going on for nearly six years, with much of it concentrated in Iraq. Many military commanders will tell you that a war is usually won before it is fought. Strategy and preparation are keys to winning on the battlefield. It is no different in the spiritual realm.

Recently National Geographic published an article on the Alaska bull moose and how the males of this species go head-to-head for dominance, with antlers crunching and often breaking. Broken antlers often ensure defeat, as the heaviest and strongest moose with the biggest and most powerful antlers will win the battle.

The interesting thing about these bull moose fights is that while the actual battles take place in the fall, the preparation occurs in the summer. That's when they are eating constantly to get themselves ready for war. The bull moose who consumes the best diet for growing the biggest, strongest antlers and having the most overall bulk is going to be the most prepared and likely to win whatever encounter he is in. A weaker diet means less bulk, weaker antlers and defeat in the fall (similar to the life of a National Football League lineman).

There is a lesson here for us today. Spiritual battles await us. Satan will choose a season during which to attack; it's not a matter of if, but when. Whether you find victory or defeat depends a great deal upon what you do now in preparation for battle.

Here is what you might call the "bull moose principle" for spiritual warfare: Faith, strength and wisdom for trials are best developed before they are needed.

The book of Ephesians is a prison epistle. Paul was often chained to a Roman soldier as he wrote, so the military language in these passages should not surprise us.

The first nine verses of Ephesians 6 could be considered "boot camp training" for spiritual warfare. Verse 1-4 address children and parents, while verses 5-9 are for servants and masters or employees and employers. Those passages lead into verse 10-18, which address spiritual warfare more directly. This is an ongoing war, and we are to be prepared and armed to fight every day, as the bull moose in Alaska must be.

There are two primary considerations in this military-style preparation. You should be concerned with who your **enemy** is and what **equipment** is needed to fight that enemy.

The enemy is identified in verses 10-13. *"Finally, my brethren, be strong in the Lord, and in the power of his might. Put on the whole armour of God, that ye may be able to stand against the wiles of the devil. For we wrestle not against flesh and blood, but against principalities, against powers, against the rulers of the darkness of this world, against spiritual wickedness in high places. Wherefore take unto you the whole armour of God, that ye may be able to withstand in the evil day, and having done all, to stand."*

You need to know and respect your enemy. He is powerful. The warfare described in these verses is a life-and-death fight to the finish. The beautiful thing, as verse 10 indicates, is that we receive strength from Christ to fight this fight.

Some of you may be wondering why we have to know this enemy and fight this battle. Many who profess Christ even say, according to research from George Barna and others, that they believe the devil is a myth – a colorful figure with horns and a pitchfork. No, he is very real, he is powerful, and there are five reasons why you need to be on the lookout for him.

First, according to Luke 11:15, he is the ruler of demons. Spiritual warfare is a reality, and Satan is the commander-in-chief of the principalities and powers of the air.

Second, according to 2 Cor. 4:4, he is the god (small "g") of this world. He has been tolerated by God (capital "G") in His economy. Sin was brought into the world through the temptation of Satan as the serpent in Genesis 3, and God has permitted him to exist in this world as a part of His perfect plan for redemption.

In John 8:44, when Jesus addressed the scribes and Pharisees who questioned His authority, He told them, "*Ye are of your father the devil.*" Those are harsh words coming from the Lord. Satan inspires and influences you, and he tempts you to sin. Simply put, he is your dad if you do not know Christ. This seems like hard-core stuff, but it is true and you need to know it if you are to be prepared to fight the enemy.

Third, he is the prince of the power of the air. Eph. 2:2 says, "*Wherein in time past ye walked according to the course of this world, according to the prince of the power of the air, the spirit that now worketh in the children of disobedience.*"

Before you came to Christ, whatever age that was, you walked with your father the devil. Under the sovereign view and reign of God, he was moving you and influencing you to do things that you should not have been doing.

Fourth, as I John 5:19 tells us, the whole world lies within his power. He is a powerful tempter, often using the lust of the flesh, the lust of the eyes and the pride of life as his weapons, according to I John 2.

You need to know these things so you can have a proper perspective of your enemy. On one extreme are those who consider the devil just a mythological figure, and on the other extreme are those who see Satan around every corner and in every face they pass by on the street. They behave as though they want to face off with him at any time. That's not the way to go, either.

C.S. Lewis' classic book "The Screwtape Letters," written about the time of World War II, is a fascinating fictional allegory

197

of the relationship Satan has with this world. The main characters are a demonic creature known as Screwtape and his apprentice, Wormwood. The story is an account of how God allows Satan to work subtly within the lives of people with temptation. Here is what Lewis said about the perspective of his book:

"There are two equal and opposite errors into which our race can fall about the devils. One is to disbelieve in their existence, and the other is to believe and feel an excessive and unhealthy interest in them. They [the demons] themselves are equally pleased by both errors, and hail a materialist or a magician with the same delight."

You want to respect your enemy. You don't want to initiate battle with him, and you certainly don't want to dismiss him as nothing more than a myth.

Fifth, he is deceptive. Consider in Eph. 6:11 the phrase *"the wiles of the devil."* That is an interesting choice of words. Other translations may include the word *"schemes,"* and the root word used here refers to a method or a strategy. That's how he works. Satan disguises himself as an angel of light, according to 2 Cor. 11:14. He is *diablos*, which literally means "deceiver." He is the great liar.

The Bible says in Eph. 5:11 that it is our job to expose his strategies, so now I will give you a handbook of Satan's schemes. This is not an all-inclusive list, but here are some top choices.

Satan is the father of lies, according to John 8. He works very subtly.

He opposes the Word of God by doubting its authorship, its accuracy and its acceptability. A great illustration of this is in the account of the fall of man in Gen. 3. The deceiver comes upon Eve and Adam in concert, after they have received instructions by direct revelation from God to enjoy themselves in the Garden of Eden except for one thing they are forbidden to do. The serpent is allowed to come on the scene, and he starts by obscuring the Word of God.

"That's not what He meant," he says. "You're not going to die just by eating that fruit. There are only two of you. Besides, don't you want to have the same knowledge as God and know all about good and evil? God is holding you back." That's the deception.

Another of Satan's schemes is that he tries to slow missions. He would do all he can to stop those who would minister and share the Word of God to ready and available ears across the country and around the world. He is not thrilled with anyone who is doing that. In Acts 13:8-9 he used a magician in an attempt to stop Paul and Silas from preaching to a government leader in Cyprus.

Satan also uses the fear of death. Have you ever noticed on a death bed the difference between someone who is ready to meet God and someone who is not? A saved person has the attitude, "Take me home; to be absent from the body is to be present with the Lord; to die is gain." That was Paul's attitude. He couldn't wait to go.

But with an unbeliever, it is very sad to be around the family at the time of death. I have seen people at funerals who don't know where their loved one is or whether they will see each other again. They have questions like, "Is this all there is? Am I just going to end up as food for worms? Is there an eternity?" That kind of thinking is hard to live with. But Satan loves it, and he tried to put that doubt into the heart of a Christian as well.

Another of his methods is that he blinds unbelievers from the truth. If you have recently come to Christ, think about the times you studied and read the Bible before you were saved. Do you ever wonder why it didn't make sense to you? It is the work of Satan as illustrated in 2 Cor. 4:4. "In *whom the god of this world hath blinded the minds of them which believe not, lest the light of the glorious gospel of Christ, who is the image of God, should shine unto them.*"

God is the One who takes the blinders off. He transforms and regenerates your heart at the appointed time, but before that, if you don't know Christ, very little of the Bible makes any sense to you. It's just literature, like any other book.

I remember the first time I read it after coming to Christ. It was like a light coming on. I finally understood what I couldn't understand before, because the natural man does not discern the things of God.

Satan also imitates signs and wonders. The Bible says in 2 Thess. 2:9, "Even him, whose coming is after the working of Satan with all power and signs and lying wonders."

I spoke to someone recently about a grandmother who has been seeing apparitions, with people appearing out of nowhere. Often you have heard of our Roman Catholic friends who see Mary appear in the most unusual places. Who is bringing this about?

Satan brings persecution. He has never stopped doing that. More Christians were martyred in the twentieth century than in the previous 1,900 years. It didn't end four or five hundred years ago as some people might think. It is happening today in places like Sudan, where slavery is legal and Christians are held in bondage, and many Islamic countries where one must go underground or risk death to preach and share the gospel. The book of Revelation indicates that more of this is on the way.

Satan brings sickness. In Luke 13:16 Jesus reprimanded some skeptics regarding a disabled woman He healed: *"And ought not this woman, being a daughter of Abraham, whom Satan hath bound, lo, these eighteen years, be loosed from this bond on the sabbath day?"*

You are probably familiar with the story of Job, which is the classic scenario. His body ravaged by illness, his family wiped out – that was Satanic warfare at work.

Satan brings sexual temptation. I Cor. 7:5 says, "Defraud ye not one the other, except it be with consent for a time, that ye may give yourselves to fasting and prayer; and come together again, that Satan tempt you not for your incontinency."

Finally, consider Satan's very first act, which is to tempt in the area of pride. Look at I Tim. 3:6. *"Not a novice, lest being lifted up with pride he fall into the condemnation of the devil."*

Lucifer was the most beautiful, powerful being created before Genesis 1 in all of history. But it wasn't enough. "I want to be like God," he said. Pride and ego led to his downfall.

It was the same for Adam and Eve. What a great deal they had in the Garden of Eden, and they threw it all away. But we can't just dump on them, because good theology indicates that they were representative of the entire human race. Any of us, in the same situation, would have done the same thing.

C.S. Lewis, in the "The Screwtape Letters," said, "The safest road to hell is the gradual one – the gentle slope, soft under foot, without sudden turnings, without milestones, without signposts."

Satan is very subtle. He doesn't come at you face-to-face like something out of a movie. Look at Eph. 6:12. *"For we wrestle not against flesh and blood, but against principalities, against powers, against the rulers of the darkness of this world, against spiritual wickedness in high places."*

Notice the plural words used throughout that verse. It means that Satan has reinforcements with which to battle against you and me. He is not omniscient, omnipresent or omnipotent, but he has an army of demons and other tools at his disposal to compensate for that.

Just as Satan has schemes, God has equipment to protect us from Satan's devices. This equipment is callled the armor of God.

What I love about this equipment is that Jesus will be wearing it when He returns. The book of Isaiah says that He will wear the whole armor of God as the redeemer of Zion. In fact, we find a parallel of our passage from Ephesians in Is. 59:17. *"For he put on righteousness as a breastplate, and an helmet of salvation upon his head; and he put on the garments of vengeance for clothing, and was clad with zeal as a cloak."* That verse talks about Jesus Christ.

But before He even wears it, we have access to that armor now. We just have to remember to put it on and wear it as Christians.

Looking at the pieces that comprise the full armor of God, we first see three items that were worn at all times on the battleground, followed by three pieces that were to be ready to use at a moment's notice.

Look at Eph. 6:14. *"Stand therefore, having your loins girt about with truth, and having on the breastplate of righteousness."*

The first item is the belt of truth. A belt was important in battle because of the long robes men wore at this time, which could get them tangled up easily if they were not held in place. Also, the middle region of the male body was known as the "power of regeneration," so it was important for a male soldier to "gird his loins" to prepare for battle.

What is truth? This question is important because so many in today's society are prone to say, "Well, your truth is your truth and my truth is my truth."

But there is such a thing as absolute truth, regardless of whether people want to admit it. The law of gravity is one example of this. It cannot be debated or contested. Likewise, it might make me feel better to imagine that two plus two equals five, but it will never happen. Reality tells us that it is always four.

The Son of God came on the scene 2,000 years ago and said, "*I am the way, the truth, and the life: no man cometh unto the Father, but by me.*" (John 14:6) That is not negotiable for the Christian. There is no such thing as negotiating the reality of Jesus Christ, which is why Acts 4:12 tells us, "*Neither is there salvation in any other: for there is none other name under heaven given among men, whereby we must be saved.*"

All roads do not lead to God any more than all roads lead to Walt Disney World or to my house. There is only one way leading into the Kingdom and that is Jesus Christ. That is why we should always be girded with the belt of truth.

The second part of verse 14 talks about the breastplate of righteousness. The breastplate is a two-sided piece connected from the neck to the waist, which is very important for protection of the vital organs from spears that fly through the air in battle.

In this verse it symbolizes our righteous life in Christ. The beautiful thing about salvation is that you are justified and declared righteous before God because Christ's sinless life is put on your account. But if we have that, we need to walk that way and live like it, and the more we are living like sold-out disciples of Jesus, the harder it is for the fiery darts of the enemy to penetrate us. When you purpose in your heart to live out the Word and not just believe it, you are putting on the breastplate of righteousness.

Now look at verse 15. "*And your feet shod with the preparation of the gospel of peace.*" The shoes worn by soldiers in Bible times had spikes similar to what football players might wear today, to give them firm footing during hand-to-hand combat in the field. The idea here for us is that, when you are following the Great Commission and sharing Christ with others, you will know a peace that allows God to speak through you.

We are simply God's messengers; we do not save anyone. But you can be witnessing to someone and suddenly realize that you are sounding like John the Baptist. That's because God is giving you exactly what He wants you to say when you are wearing the shoes of the gospel of peace.

The Christian life consists of three great marching orders from God: the Great Commandment (to love the Lord with all your heart, soul, mind and strength, and love your neighbor as yourself); the Great Commission (to go and make disciples of all nations, baptizing and teaching them); and the Great Commitment (to follow Acts 1:8 and be witnesses here and around the world). These are not optional. We need to be equipped for these tasks in the most comprehensive way possible, and that is by taking on the armor we are talking about in this passage.

The remaining items needed for battle are covered in verses 16-17. *"Above all, taking the shield of faith, wherewith ye shall be able to quench all the fiery darts of the wicked. And take the helmet of salvation, and the sword of the Spirit, which is the word of God."*

The shield used during the time Paul wrote this verse was usually oblong, about two feet by four feet, and it even contained leather that would absorb and extinguish the fiery darts that were shot by the opposing army.

The helmet is obviously important because it protects your head. This helmet is referred to in I Thess. 5:8 as the helmet of *"the hope of salvation."* It is talking about eternal security and assurance, a beautiful promise of God.

If God is powerful enough to save you, I would submit that He is also powerful enough to keep you. Also, as Matt. 6 points out, we who are in Christ should not worry about our basic material needs, because if God can save you and keep you, He can take care of three meals a day and a roof over your head.

Jesus said in John 6:37, *"All that the Father giveth me shall come to me; and him that cometh to me I will in no wise cast out. ... And this is the Father's will which hath sent me, that of all which he hath given me I should lose nothing, but should raise it up again at the last day."* That is your hope.

For the unbeliever, hope is simply wishing for a better car or house or for more money. For the Christian, hope is an unrealized true expectancy of something. We are waiting, with great anticipation and expectation, for the Second Coming of Christ. We know it's true, and we are ready for it, as John was when he said in Rev. 22:20, *"Even so, come, Lord Jesus."* That was 2,000 years ago, but the Lord *"is longsuffering to us-ward, not willing that any should perish, but that all should come to repentance."* (2 Pet. 3:9) So we are to continue doing His work until He comes.

Two verses that are a powerful as any for use as ammunition against the enemy are found in Rom. 8:38-39, which Paul wrote from prison. *"For I am persuaded, that neither death, nor life, nor angels, nor principalities, nor powers, nor things present, nor things to come, Nor height, nor depth, nor any other creature, shall be able to separate us from the love of God, which is in Christ Jesus our Lord."*

That is a promise. You can take it to the bank. Either all of the Bible is true or none of it is true. You have to know that. It is a weapon.

The last piece of armor mentioned in Eph. 6:17 is *"the sword of the Spirit, which is the word of God."* There were different types of swords in the days of the gladiators. One of them was a hacking sword which you could use to take a man's head off. But the sword in this verse is actually a dagger about 6-18 inches long and is used for hand-to-hand combat. In fact, it may have been the sword Peter used in the Garden of Gethsemane to slice off the servant's ear when the soldiers came to arrest Jesus, since the larger sword would have likely caused much more damage.

The sword mentioned in this verse is the only weapon described in the Bible that is offensive, not defensive. You can lead with it and use it to advance.

The sword of the Spirit is described in Heb. 4:12 this way: *"For the word of God is quick, and powerful, and sharper than any two-edged sword, piercing even to the dividing asunder of soul and spirit, and of the joints and marrow, and is a discerner of the thoughts and intents of the heart."*

That is your Bible. It is not just any book. It is a supernatural book containing the greatest news in the history of the world, which is that Jesus saves sinners.

There is perhaps no better illustration in the Bible of using the helmet of salvation, the shield of faith and the sword of the Spirit than what is found in Matthew 4. Jesus had fasted for 40 days and was hungry, since He was man as well as God. We see in these verses the need for Scripture meditation and memorization to help us win in our battles with the enemy.

The first instance is in verses 3-4. *"And when the tempter came to him, he said, If thou be the Son of God, command that these stones be made bread. But he answered and said, It is written, Man shall not live by bread alone, but by every word that proceedeth out of the mouth of God."*

Note the words *"it is written."* Jesus took Deut. 8:3 and used it against Satan. Strike one.

Now look at verses 5-7. *"Then the devil taketh him up into the holy city, and setteth him on a pinnacle of the temple, And saith unto him, If thou be the Son of God, cast thyself down: for it is written, He shall give his angels charge concerning thee: and in their hands they shall bear thee up, lest at any time thou dash thy foot against a stone. Jesus said unto him, It is written again, Thou shalt not tempt the Lord thy God."*

Satan uses Scripture here, quoting from Psalm 91:11-12, albeit an incorrect interpretation. But Christ comes back again with the Word, specifically Deut. 6:16, and takes another whack with the sword of the Spirit. Strike two.

Finally, Satan took one last swing in verses 8-9. *"Again, the devil taketh him up into an exceeding high mountain, and sheweth him all the kingdoms of the world, and the glory of them; And saith unto him, All these things will I give thee, if thou wilt fall down and worship me."*

With these words, Satan was essentially telling Christ that He did not have to go to the cross. But Jesus struck the final blow in verses 10-11.

"Then saith Jesus unto him, Get thee hence, Satan: for it is written, Thou shalt worship the Lord thy God, and him only shalt thou serve. Then the devil leaveth him, and, behold, angels came and ministered unto him."

This sword is for us to use as Christians. Hebrews 12 tells us that we all have besetting sins, those "pet peeve" sins that we can't seem to get past. They range from gluttony to sexual temptation and everywhere in between. Satan is powerful, and this is where he attacks you. He will hit you day in and day out at your weakest point.

Satan spends more time on Christians than on unbelievers, of whom he is already the father. He works on Christians to break their witness and their testimony, because if you are going to church every Sunday and sinning throughout the week, people see that. The Christian life is 24 hours a day, seven days a week, and 365 days a year.

Paul sums up everything in verse 18 of Ephesians 6 and actually provides an extra weapon which is often overlooked. *"Praying always with all prayer and supplication in the Spirit, and watching thereunto with all perseverance and supplication for all saints."*

Are you praying for your brothers and sisters in Christ, that they would have victory over the enemy in spiritual warfare? Are you helping them put on the armor of God?

Prayer is the preferred and most powerful tool at our disposal. We need prayer warriors in this spiritual warfare.

The Syrophenician mother in Mark 7 went after Jesus, when He was tired and looking to rest, and would not let Him go until He cast demons out of her daughter. A parable in Luke tells of a woman who woke up a judge in the middle of the night and bugged him until he finally gave her the answers she needed.

The book of Hebrews tells us that we have access to the throne and we don't need a confessional booth or a priest. We have Jesus. According to I Tim. 2:5, *"For there is one God, and one mediator between God and men, the man Christ Jesus."* You can talk to your Father and King every day. What an honor and privilege. But what are we doing with it?

CHAPTER 20

WHAT MATTERS MOST
Ephesians 6:19-24

—⚬⚬—

If I was to ask you today to write down three of four things that really matter in life, what would they be?

Back in Ephesians 1, we found three special forms of protection in the Father, Son and Holy Spirit. God is the Father of all of us who are saved. It is His Son who has redeemed us and by whom our sins are forgiven; we are brought into the family of God by Him. The work of the Holy Spirit seals us unto the day of redemption. Through all of this we have this great new identity which is so thrilling.

Paul writes in that first chapter about how we are see through our Father's eyes, how we embrace God's plan for our lives, how He has changed us and we keep our attention on Him. If you are a child of God, the Father looks at you through Jesus Christ and sees you as if you had never committed a sin in your life.

We learn in the second chapter of Ephesians about a special gift. We are dead without Christ, but through Him we are made alive. Perhaps the most important two words in this entire book are "but God." That phrase is repeated in Ephesians 2 to illustrate how God, in His mercy and redemptive power, has given us something we never could have acquired anywhere else. From that, He works and weaves our lives into what He wants us to be, regardless of our past,

God's new society is proclaimed in the third chapter, which shows how race and background are irrelevant when it comes to entering the family of God. Chapter four stresses the importance of unity and how we make up the body of Christ with our individual gifts, while emphasizing that we walk with the goal of not hurting God.

We found in Ephesians 5 that we are to follow God, walk in the Spirit, and order our private lives accordingly. Character, repentance and renewal are among the important themes found in this passage, with everything pointing to the absolute necessity of being filled with the Spirit, which affects our marriages and family lives in such a positive way as we grow closer to each other as a result of getting closer to Christ.

The responsibility of fathers, workplace relationships and the full armor of God are key components of the sixth chapter, leading to the final few verses of Paul's great letter to the Ephesians, where we examine what matters most in life.

Life is constantly changing. My wife and I recently celebrated 40 years of marriage as well as 40 years in the ministry. That journey began in 1967, when Lyndon Johnson was president and Hubert Humphrey was vice president.

According to the book "The Year That Was: 1967," the population of the United States was 198 million people, and 3.4 billion people lived on Earth at that time.

President Johnson earned $100,000 per year, while one of the top entertainers in the country at that time, Johnny Carson, earned a whopping $1 million per year as the host of NBC's "Tonight Show." The average major league baseball player earned a $19,000 annual salary, and the federal minimum wage was $1.40 per hour.

At the grocery store in 1967, bacon was 90 cents a pound, a loaf of bread cost 22 cents and eggs were 49 cents a dozen. A Hershey chocolate bar (which comes straight from Heaven, in case you didn't know) cost a nickel.

Tickets for a Jefferson Airplane concert ranged from $3 to $5, while a Broadway performance of "Hello, Dolly!" was less than $10 for the most expensive seats. Purchasing a Corvair coupe, which was a major statement of how cool you were, would set you back

$2,100 – but for less than $5,000 you could have a Porsche 912. Of course, keeping them on the road was no problem with gasoline at 28 cents per gallon.

The average home price in the United States was $24,600 and a first-class stamp cost a nickel. That was in 1967. Things have changed a little, haven't they?

As I read these facts and thought about how much things change, I began to consider what really matters in life. Before I read that book, if you had asked me about any of the information I just listed with the possible exception of the president and vice president, I probably would not have been able to tell you any of it. So what really matters?

I believe that at the end of the book of Ephesians, the Apostle Paul gives us a few things that matter. Now we have already come up with some obvious answers, such as "The Lord matters" or "My family matters," but we need to look beyond those things as well.

In verse 21, Paul suggests that friends really matter. *"But that ye also may know my affairs, and how I do, Tychicus, a beloved brother and faithful minister in the Lord, shall make known to you all things."*

Paul wrote this epistle from jail, and he wanted people to know how he was doing. His friend Tychicus helped him do that.

What do we know about Tychicus? He was mentioned in the book of Colossians, and also in Acts 20:4, where we find that he was a native of Asia Minor. He and Oenesimus carried the epistles to the Ephesians and Colossians and also a letter to the Laodecians. He was one of the men chosen to accompany Paul and take a financial gift from the Gentile churches to Jerusalem. He was cited in 2 Tim. 4:12 and Titus 3:12 as a messenger of God.

But in this passage he has the title of *"beloved brother."* When we accept Christ as Saviour, we gain many brothers and sisters in Christ. But occasionally we acquire a beloved brother, one who is so important to us that sometimes he or she is closer than our natural family members.

Stop and think. Are you a Tychicus to someone today? We all know of friendships that don't end well. If you hope to have friends in life, you have to be forgiving to people. You think, "So-and-so was my friend until he failed me in this situation," but there are probably times you have failed him as well.

As we go through this journey in life, no man is an island unto himself. We need people who will come into our lives and be our friends.

But Tychicus not only has the title of Paul's beloved brother, but he is referred to as a *"faithful minister."* The word "minister" here means "servant" and is from the same Greek word that gives us the word "deacon." He was devoted to the service of God and a helper to the Apostle Paul. He was used to relieve Paul's restrictions to further the Kingdom of God. We hear often about Paul and other key characters in the Bible, but rarely hear about the people like Tychicus.

Paul also informs us in these verses about Tychicus' task. That is detailed in the latter portion of verse 21 and continues in verse 22: *"Whom I have sent unto you for the same purpose, that ye might know our affairs, and that he might comfort your hearts."*

Tychicus was charged with bringing people information about Paul. There were concerns about his health and his legal troubles, since he was in prison at this writing. Someone might want to know if he had a good lawyer or if his finances were sufficient.

Paul's friends also were likely to inquire about the people he won to Christ while in prison, since he did that on a regular basis no matter where he was.

The last phrase of verse 22 gives us a view of Tychicus' tenderness. He understood the situation.

Acts 20 gives an account of how Paul ministered to the Ephesians, going door to door and spreading the gospel. Lives were changed and the people grew to love him dearly. When Paul determined that he should move on, they reacted with sorrow, as expressed in verses 37-38. *"And they all wept sore, and fell on Paul's neck, and kissed him, Sorrowing most of all for the words which he spake, that they should see his face no more. And they accompanied him unto the ship."*

You can almost see them standing on the shore, with tears in their eyes, until the ship disappears over the horizon. Many of those

standing at the dock were won to Christ and taught about the Word
of God by Paul

So when he later is in prison and writing to the Ephesians, they
want to know about his condition. They get their wish and are thrilled
when Tychicus comes with the news, because he is a man they know
will give them accurate information.

While Paul had his troubles, even to the point of prison, he was
triumphing in this passage. He was looking to the future. That's
the wonderful thing about being a child of God. Your next step can
always be your best step, and someday your next step will be from
this life into eternity and the presence of God.

Once you are in His presence, you will not want to come back.
I had an evangelist friend, Curtis Hutson, who was dying of cancer
when someone asked him if he was afraid of dying. "I don't know,"
he said. "I've never died before."

What a great answer. So many of us have a fear of death because
we love what is here, especially the people we care about here. But
one day we will see Him, and that will mean more than anything
else.

As you look at the relationship between Paul and Tychicus, think
about the kind of friend you are. Who are your friends? Who are the
people you can trust and who really trust you?

Having friends in life is important, and we become friends by
giving of ourselves to others. Tychicus was a man of friendship.

Time magazine published a lengthy article in July of 2007 entitled "How We Get Addicted." One of the scientists quoted in the
story, Dr. Nora Volkow, defines addiction this way: "Addiction has a
specific definition. You are unable to stop when you want to, despite
being aware of the adverse consequences. It permeates your life.
You spend more and more time satisfying that craving."

This same article lists the major addictions in the United States,
in no particular order: alcohol; drugs (led by marijuana, cocaine and
pain relievers); tobacco; caffeine (the most common mood-altering
drug in the world, routinely ingested by 80-90 percent of Americans
through soft drinks and coffee); food (affects up to four million
American adults and leads to depression); gambling (up to 10
million adults in the U.S. are problem gamblers); shopping (which

affects both genders almost equally); sex (the least-understood of all addictions, although 16 million Americans may be affected); and the Internet.

After reading that list, consider this: Are there some things we should be addicted to? I would suggest that Paul, in finishing the book of Ephesians, is reminding us that there are some things we should be addicted to. You might call them fruit, as seen by characteristics in our lives.

Look at verse 23. *"Peace be to the brethren, and love with faith, from God the Father and the Lord Jesus Christ."* The three traits to which we should be addicted are peace, grace and love.

Notice that Paul cited a specific directive for peace, not peace to the whole world or even the peace of Jerusalem, although we should pray for that. *"Peace to the brethren"* is a recurring theme in Paul's writings. He wrote in Eph. 2:14, *"For he is our peace."* Our peace is found in none other than Jesus Christ. When we accept Christ we have peace with God the Father through Christ.

Phil. 4:7 says, *"And the peace of God, which passeth all understanding, shall keep your hearts and minds through Christ Jesus."*

Col. 3:15 says, "And let the peace of God rule in your hearts, to the which also ye are called in one body; and be ye thankful."

So we see in Paul's epistles a constant theme of peace. We know that in this world around us there is a raging war, and Satan does not want you to be at peace. But there is a responsibility among Christians to be at peace with their brothers and sisters.

We're OK with that until someone has a problem with our doctrine (not cardinal doctrine). Then our attitude is, "I'm right and you're wrong." This attitude also carries over into some of the things we practice.

Watch how Satan works on us and where he strikes. So many times it is his attempt to get us tangled up regarding our peace with one another.

I have a responsibility before God to be at peace with you. You have a responsibility before God to be at peace with me. If we fail to live like that, we lose the anointing that God has for our lives.

Jerry Vines, a noted evangelist and long-time pastor, defines anointing this way: "It is a special touch for a special task." I don't know what it is, but God has given you a special task. It changes from time to time, and you find it as you follow Him. He also gives you a special touch for it, but when we are not at peace with people, we lose that touch from God.

The second addiction we need is grace. It is the unmerited and undeserved favor of God that shines on us and sets our feet to salvation. Note that this grace in verse 23 is from God the Father – not God the Judge, but God the Creator.

Third, there is love. In this verse it is listed with faith. This love is not a sentimental love or a wishy-washy love, but it comes from the Master with sincerity and without any corruption. It is a love that brings us face-to-face with Christ.

In our church, as I'm sure is the case in your church, there are numerous ministry opportunities for us each and every week. When we have the love of the Lord in our lives, we want to be involved in serving Him. If there is anything we should be addicted to, it is the Person of Jesus Christ.

Addiction is not wrong when it is put into the proper perspective. Some people will say, "Don't get too wild and crazy about your faith." I thank God for people who are crazy about their faith when it is true, right and real.

The first five words of verse 23 are important. *"Peace be to the brethren"* refers to your family – not your biological family, but the family of God.

Many of the points Paul makes in Ephesians are personal. Eph. 1:3 says, *"Blessed be the God and Father of our Lord Jesus Christ, who hath blessed us with all spiritual blessings in heavenly places in Christ."* That is our personal relationship with God, and it is also spotlighted in Eph. 5:21, which says, *"Submitting yourselves one to another in the fear of God."*

But there is also the corporate side. Eph. 1:1 says, *"Paul, an apostle of Jesus Christ by the will of God, to the saints which are at Ephesus, and to the faithful in Christ Jesus."* He is referring to the body of Christ. There is a brotherhood that God draws us into so that we can be as one before Him. The family of God is a wonderful thing.

My wife and I got home late on a Friday night after a recent vacation. We got to bed about 11 p.m. and were awakened by the phone at 4 a.m. The caller ID read, "Unknown caller." I decided not to answer it, thinking it was probably someone in California who wanted to sell us something and got the time zones mixed up.

The same thing happened at 6 a.m. and we ignored it again. A few hours later we were drinking our morning coffee (with that addictive caffeine) when it rang a third time. I suggested to my wife that she answer it and tell the caller we were not interested.

It was not a salesperson on the line, but a lady from London named Anna Pedone, who is a cousin of mine. "We've been looking for you," she said to me when I got on the phone.

She was from Avaniano, Italy, and she began telling me about where my parents were raised and where her parents raised. "We want to start connecting with you and build a relationship with you," she said.

"Wow," I said to myself as I thought about this newfound connection that began in Italy and ran through England to reach me. "That's what a family can be like."

But as exceptional as that is, it's not anything like the joy of the family of God.

Some of us are smart and some are not. Some of us are good-looking and some are not. Some have great athletic ability and some do not. Some like the New York Yankees and others like the Boston Red Sox. We are all different, but we can all be part of the family of God.

So what matters most? We know that friends matter, the fruits of following God matter, and the family of God matters.

After taking this great epistle verse by verse over these pages, I want to give you what I believe are two things that will sum up the book of Ephesians.

First, live according to what God has done for you.

Perhaps the greatest apologist of the twentieth century was C.S. Lewis. In "Paralandra," the protagonist says to his friend Ransom after returning from another planet, "A man who has been in another world does not come back unchanged." As we see who and what we are in Christ according to the book of Ephesians, let's strive to be different.

Second, may all who come behind us find us faithful.

On a recent Saturday we had a beautiful service during which a couple in our church renewed their vows for their 25th anniversary. All of their children took part. Afterward, the husband said to me, "I really did this for my children. I wanted them to see a couple, married 25 years, still in love."

Things change over the years, but there are some things that really matter in life. I want to challenge all of us to take these things and apply them to our lives.

Phil. 3:13-14 says, *"Brethren, I count not myself to have apprehended: but this one thing I do, forgetting those things which are behind, and reaching forth unto those things which are before, I press toward the mark for the prize of the high calling of God in Christ Jesus."*

Many years ago there was an Olympic qualifying event whose participants included Jim Ryun, a believer and the greatest runner in the world at that time. No one could run the mile like him, and he was a shoo-in to win this race.

As the race was in its early stages, suddenly Ryun collided with another runner and fell to the ground. The remainder of the field took off ahead of him, and he would never win the race.

Banged up, he got to his feet. Most of the crowd thought he would walk off the track, but instead he started running as fast as he could. He came in dead last, but he finished the race and won the hearts of millions by not giving up.

That's what we are called to do. As we think about all of the great things God has done for us, let's go out and finish the race well. As you do, you will touch the heart of God.

LPSIA information can be obtained at www.ICGtesting.com
Printed in the USA
BVOW022335211111
276553BV00003B/1/P